PRAISE FOR
THE EMOTIONAL INTELLIGENCE BOOK

"Looking to lower your stress levels, build healthy relationships, adopt a positive mindset and bounce back from setbacks? Then this book is for you! Nicole has personally helped me to develop an emotionally intelligent approach to my career, which in turn is helping me lead a more meaningful life."

ANNA MARIA BLENGINO
CIO, Sunrise

"All too often we focus on people's academic ability or technical skills – this book is a powerful reminder of the crucial role emotional intelligence plays in setting you up for success in your personal and professional life."

BELLAMY FORD
Director of Disputes, Taylor Rose

"As Nicole points out in this inspiring book – life is not a dress rehearsal. Whatever your stage of life, follow her excellent advice to help you achieve your full potential."

KITTA VIRTAVUO

CPO, F-secure Corporation

"Nicole's deep expertise, passion for coaching and extensive experience shines through in this practical guide to harnessing the power of emotional intelligence."

LYNDA LOGAN

Chief Revenue Officer, Reorg

"An excellent introduction to the importance of emotional intelligence. This book will equip you with the tools you need to build your emotional intelligence skills so you can effectively manage the ebb and flow of life."

MARK THORPE

CEO & Managing Director, Operations, KP Snacks

"If you don't know what you want or how to ask for it, you won't get it. I highly recommend you read The Emotional Intelligence Book to dial up your ambition, self-confidence and achieve the outcomes you deserve."

TAMARA GILLAN

Founder and CEO of The WealthiHer Network

FOR OTHER TITLES
IN THE SERIES...

CONCISE
ADVICE
LAB

SMALL BOOKS: BIG IDEAS

CLEVER CONTENT, DYNAMIC IDEAS, PRACTICAL
SOLUTIONS AND ENGAGING VISUALS –
A CATALYST TO INSPIRE NEW WAYS OF THINKING
AND PROBLEM-SOLVING IN A COMPLEX WORLD

www.lidpublishing.com/product-category/concise-advice-series

Published by
LID Publishing
An imprint of LID Business Media Ltd.
LABS House, 15-19 Bloomsbury Way,
London, WC1A 2TH, UK

info@lidpublishing.com
www.lidpublishing.com

A member of:

BPR ◉
businesspublishersroundtable.com

© Nicole Soames, 2023
© LID Business Media Limited, 2023
Reprinted in 2024

Printed by Imak Ofset

ISBN: 978-1-911687-85-6
ISBN: 978-1-911687-86-3 (ebook)

Cover and page design: Caroline Li

THE EMOTIONAL INTELLIGENCE BOOK

HOW TO DEVELOP YOUR EQ
FOR A MORE SUCCESSFUL LIFE

NICOLE SOAMES

MADRID | MEXICO CITY | LONDON
BUENOS AIRES | BOGOTA | SHANGHAI

CONTENTS

INTRODUCTION

1. WHAT IS EMOTIONAL INTELLIGENCE?

The aim of this book is to awaken your curiosity about the power of emotional intelligence in everyday life. Only then can you truly understand why emotional intelligence is your biggest differentiator and the secret to setting you up for success. It doesn't matter what your job title says you do – we all need emotional intelligence to be able to understand ourselves, influence others, and gain the right perspective and future focus. It's about taking practical steps to enhance your emotional intelligence skills and infuse them with your other skills so you can be truly successful in the everyday ebb and flow of life for now and for always.

The first step is to clarify what is meant by the term emotional intelligence, or EQ. **Emotional intelligence is defined as a set of emotional and social skills that are most effective at influencing others. In other words, it's the ability to recognize and manage your own emotions and those of others.** The term was first made popular in 1995 by psychologist Daniel Goleman in his book *Emotional Intelligence*. Goleman highlighted the importance of emotional intelligence when he said, "If your emotional abilities aren't in hand, if you don't have self-awareness, if you are not able to manage your distressing emotions, if you can't have effective relationships, then no matter how smart you are, you are not going to get very far."[1] His research laid the foundation for much of the theory about emotional intelligence today. Since then, the concept of emotional intelligence has captured everyone's imagination, including mine! Whether it's online quizzes to test your emotional intelligence or the proliferation of articles about it in the press, you could be forgiven for assuming emotional intelligence is here to solve all our problems. However, emotional intelligence is no quick fix or magic pill. To understand its real impact, we need to start by debunking some of the most common myths about it.

MYTH #1: YOU'RE EITHER BORN WITH EMOTIONAL INTELLIGENCE OR YOU'RE NOT

While some people have naturally higher levels of emotional intelligence than others, the great news is that unlike your IQ, which is fairly fixed from about the age of 17, your emotional intelligence can be developed over time. Our innate level of emotional intelligence gradually rises in our late teens, developing in our 20s and 30s before peaking in our mid-50s – but these are the natural levels. By actively focusing on building your emotional intelligence as a skill set, you can increase it over time. It's like a muscle – the more you use it, the stronger it will become.

MYTH #2: EMOTIONAL INTELLIGENCE IS ALL ABOUT HAVING EMPATHY

There is a common misconception that developing your emotional intelligence is about being nice or showing empathy. While empathy is undoubtedly a key emotional intelligence skill, it is only one of many. It's also important not to confuse empathy with sympathy. Empathy is about understanding what makes someone really tick, which is different from being 'nice' to someone. People often have tunnel vision when they think of emotional intelligence and focus purely on the relationship skills. In fact, skills such as self-control, self-reliance and self-actualization are just as important to achieving success in life.

MYTH #3: WOMEN ARE NATURALLY BETTER AT EMOTIONAL INTELLIGENCE

Most people assume that women are more emotionally intelligent than men – probably because women are often better at sharing their emotions. While, as a woman, I would like to believe this, in fact women and men have equal levels of emotional intelligence. Research shows that, in general, women do score higher in empathy than their male counterparts. However, the reverse is true when it comes to measuring self-reliance and straightforwardness, where men generally fare better.[2] This is most likely explained by socialization and cultural influences as opposed to any innate differences in emotional intelligence.

MYTH #4: EMOTIONAL INTELLIGENCE IS A SET OF 'SOFT' SKILLS

So often the skills relating to emotional intelligence are mistakenly described as 'soft.' Perhaps this is because they are less tangible than other more easily measurable types of intellect or intelligence. However, emotional intelligence skills are some of the hardest to develop. This is because it takes ambition and commitment to take practical steps to change your behaviour. What makes it particularly challenging is that it involves other people. Not only do you need to manage your own emotions but you also have to constantly use your judgement and adaptability to respond to others live in the moment. No situation will ever be the same and this takes practice and hard work to master.

SO WHAT IS EMOTIONAL INTELLIGENCE REALLY?

Now that I've clarified what emotional intelligence isn't, it's time to delve deeper into exactly what it means for the purpose of this book. We will use the RocheMartin Emotional Capital Model to explore the competencies of emotional intelligence. This model is distinctive and developed from years of reseach and represents an evolution in understanding. M. Newman describes it as a set of 10 specific skills[3]. Although emotional intelligence is often described in a broad sense, it's actually a set of specific skills that will help set you up for success in life. If you look at the model below, you'll see that emotional intelligence can be broken down into four core areas. Each of these areas has specific skills you need to hone to enhance your emotional intelligence.

KNOWING YOURSELF	MANAGING YOURSELF	NAVIGATING THE WORLD AROUND YOU	MANAGING YOUR RELATIONSHIPS
SELF-AWARENESS	SELF-CONTROL SELF-CONFIDENCE SELF-RELIANCE	AMBITION ADAPTABILITY OPTIMISM SELF-ACTUALIZATION	EMPATHY RELATIONSHIP SKILLS STRAIGHTFORWARDNESS

Knowing yourself is about drawing on your self-awareness to understand what really makes you tick. It's about uncovering any blind spots so you can identify your key strengths and areas for improvement. Being genuinely motivated to improve yourself will give you the impetus you need to build your emotional intelligence. **Managing yourself** is about focusing on your own feelings and emotions so that you can control your responses to different situations, manage your mood and have the confidence to back yourself. **Navigating the world around you** refers to the set of skills that give you a sense of perspective and future focus. These include your ability to set new goals, embrace change, be solution orientated and find fulfilment. The fourth and final area is **managing your relationships**, which relates to your ability to put yourself in other people's shoes, find common ground, and build trust and respect. We will examine each of these four core areas in greater detail in the following parts of this book.

2. HOW TO SPOT PEOPLE WITH HIGH LEVELS OF EMOTIONAL INTELLIGENCE

A great way to bring these skills to life and understand the true power of emotional intelligence is to spot it in other people. Picture the last person you spent time with who made you feel really good about yourself. It could be someone at work, a friend or a member of your family. Chances are they took the time to be curious and actively listen to what you had to say. Were they positive and confident in their outlook? As a rule, we like to surround ourselves with radiators rather than drains – we prefer people whose glass is always half full, with a can-do attitude that boosts our own energy levels. After all, confidence is contagious.

Another way to spot highly emotionally intelligent people is to think of those individuals who diffuse tricky situations and deal with conflict effectively. Think of your go-to person when there's a problem. Are they cool, calm and collected in a crisis? These are the people who respond rather than react to challenging events, displaying high levels of self-control, self-reliance and straightforwardness.

By taking the time to consider the interactions you have on a daily basis, you will begin to understand how complex emotional intelligence really is and why it's so crucial to success in life.

3. WHY DOES EMOTIONAL INTELLIGENCE MATTER?

This may sound obvious, but we are human *beings,* not human *doings*. All too often we identify ourselves by the tasks we do and fail to acknowledge the impact our emotions have on our daily lives. Most of us are more emotionally driven than we realize. In fact, research shows that whether we like it or not, emotions play a critical role in our decision-making.[4] This means people make decisions based on how you make them feel and not just what you do. It's only by taking practical steps to manage your emotions and those of others that you can influence other people. This is powerfully highlighted in a quote popularly attributed to Maya Angelou: "People will forget what you said, people will forget what you did, but people will never forget how you made them feel."

Emotional intelligence is best described as a *catalyst* that will accelerate your success whatever your walk of life. Research carried out by the Carnegie Institute of Technology shows that 85% of your financial success is due to skills in 'human engineering' – your personality and your ability to communicate, negotiate and lead. Surprisingly, only 15% is due to technical knowledge or technical skills, highlighting the crucial role emotional intelligence plays in setting you up for success.[5] Given these statistics, it's not surprising that emotional intelligence has swiftly risen up the ranks of the most important skill that people can have. The benefits of having high levels of emotional intelligence are wide and encompassing, and include the following:

- You **handle stress** well. This means you function well under pressure and are skilled at balancing work and life commitments. This helps you prioritize your mental health and boost your sense of well-being.

- You **collaborate well** with others because you have highly developed social skills that allow you to get along with a diverse range of people. You understand teamwork and you seek to get the best from the people you work with.

- You are a **good listener**. Your ability to actively listen and respond to others is crucial for building strong relationships. You recognize that hearing is involuntary and listening is a skill. You 'read' beyond the words and interpret nonverbal cues to understand what really makes the other person tick.

- You are open to **feedback** and adopt a growth mentality. You see feedback as a gift that helps you to up your game, rather than acting defensively and resisting change.

- You have high levels of **empathy** (not to be confused with sympathy). You can understand other people's perspectives and are sensitive to their particular needs.

- You are seen as a **safe pair of hands** because you behave in a cool, calm and collected way. You don't get flustered and you earn respect from others by rising above daily irritations.

- You make **thoughtful and informed** decisions. You take the time to consider the outcomes of your decisions instead of acting in haste.

- You are **optimistic**. You adopt a solution-orientated approach and bounce back from setbacks by taking the learnings and moving forward.
- You have a strong **sense of fulfilment**. You understand what really motivates you in life and take practical steps to help you reach your goals.
- You achieve greater **success** in life. You are more likely to live longer and be financially better off, and are less likely to suffer from depression.

This list clearly shows how developing your emotional intelligence will help you differentiate yourself and thrive in all areas of your life, whether it's with family and friends, or in the workplace.

4. YOUR JOURNEY TO DEVELOPING YOUR EMOTIONAL INTELLIGENCE

Now that you understand the individual skills that make up emotional intelligence and why they hold the key to leading a more successful life, it's time to take practical steps to enhance your own emotional intelligence. As you journey through this book, I will break down the individual skills into bite-sized chunks and give you the tools and techniques you need to master them. Picture this book as your personal toolkit for life. As I said before, there is no magic pill. Learning and embedding new skills takes time and effort. These so-called soft skills can seem easy to learn in theory but are often hard to put into practice. Our human brains are hardwired to behave in a certain way, so we can stay in our comfort zone and stick with what we know. It's about adopting a growth mindset and believing that you are never too old to learn something new. Remember, life is not a dress rehearsal. Whatever your stage of life, you need to develop your emotional intelligence to help you achieve your potential.

The Four Stages of Competence, developed by Noel Burch,[6] is a great learning tool that can be used to explain the journey you will go on to develop your emotional intelligence skills. If you look at the starting point in the diagram below, you will see that you initially progress from **unconscious incompetence** (when you don't realize what you don't know) to **conscious incompetence** (when you know what you need to learn). This is generally the most uncomfortable phase and when you are most likely to give up. If you stay with it, you move to **conscious competence** (when you're actively trying to apply your newly developed emotional intelligence skills). The final step on your journey to becoming more emotionally intelligent is **unconscious competence**. This is when your emotional intelligence skills are second nature, regardless of the situation you find yourself in.

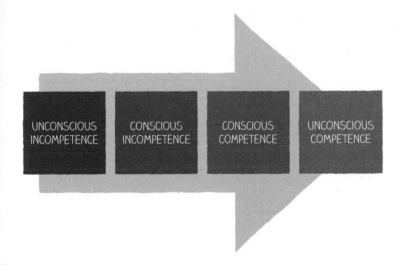

UNCONSCIOUS
INCOMPETENCE

CONSCIOUS
INCOMPETENCE

CONSCIOUS
COMPETENCE

UNCONSCIOUS
COMPETENCE

As you navigate this book, you will learn to value what you are good at (your strengths) and identify those skills you need to focus on to take them to the next level. The secret to becoming truly emotionally intelligent is to combine these skills in a balanced way so that you can perform at the best of your ability in everyday situations. This is where the 'intelligence' part comes in, as no two people or situations will be the same. It's about getting the right balance of emotional intelligence skills so that you can use your judgement to interact live in the moment. To give you an idea of how this plays out in real life, map out your week and think of all the occasions when your emotional intelligence skills come into play. It could be as a parent, a carer, a friend or a colleague. Take the time to reflect on how putting the theory into practice will help you be more successful in each of these situations. Remember, this is not just about focusing on what you *think* – it's also about identifying how you *feel* and communicate. It's only by tuning in to your emotions in this way that you can take active steps to manage your own and those of others.

KEY TAKEAWAYS

Congratulations – you've just taken your first very important step on the path to developing your emotional intelligence. Here's just a quick recap of the key points we've covered in this part of the book:

- Emotional intelligence is defined as a set of emotional and social skills that are most effective at influencing others.

- Unlike your IQ, your emotional intelligence isn't fixed and can be developed over time.

- Don't confuse having emotional intelligence with being 'nice' – emotional intelligence is about recognizing and managing your own emotions and those of others.

- Emotional intelligence can be broken down into four areas: knowing yourself, managing yourself, navigating the world around you and managing your relationships.

- Developing the set of skills in each of these four core areas will help you differentiate yourself and be successful in all areas of your life.

- People with high levels of emotional intelligence handle pressure well, collaborate effectively with others and understand people's perspectives.

- Emotionally intelligent people are more open to feedback, have a positive outlook on life and achieve a greater sense of fulfilment.
- We are all more emotionally driven than we realize – take the time to reflect on how you *feel* as well as think in the different situations you find yourself in over the course of a week.
- Putting the theory into practice can be hard – it takes ambition and commitment to change your behaviour on a daily basis.
- The practical tools and techniques in this book will help you master each emotional intelligence skill as you move along the learning pathway from unconscious incompetence to unconscious competence.
- The secret to developing your emotional intelligence is to value the skills you are good at and identify the ones you need to improve so you can achieve a sense of balance.

PART ONE

KNOWING
YOURSELF

Now that we have a clearer understanding of exactly what emotional intelligence is and why it matters, it's time to break it down into its individual components. It's only by delving deeper into each emotional intelligence skill in turn that you can take practical steps to boost your emotional intelligence levels. After all, as the saying goes, "How do you eat an elephant? In bite-sized chunks." Let's start by focusing on self-knowledge, often described as the cornerstone of emotional intelligence because it is critical for personal growth.

1. WHAT IS SELF-KNOWLEDGE?

Self-knowledge is your ability to recognize and understand your own emotions and feelings and how they influence your behaviour, judgement and decision-making. It's about developing your awareness of how your emotions and feelings impact those around you. If you don't have a sense of your own emotions and how they drive your behaviour, how can you begin to manage yourself or other people better? Developing self-knowledge is not a one-off event – it's a conscious choice to become more self-aware. According to Abraham Maslow's Hierarchy of Needs (more about him in *Part Three*), it's only by truly knowing yourself that you can find real fulfilment in life and achieve self-actualization.[7] In other words, you can't fulfil your higher needs if you don't have a foundation of emotional satisfaction.

Self-knowledge helps you identify your strengths and areas for improvement, gain clarity on your values and understand what motivates you so that you can be decisive about the actions you need to take going forward. This can be particularly challenging when you have been supressing feelings for a long time or have been masking certain emotions rather than trying to understand them. To build your awareness, you need to dig deeper and get a clearer understanding of yourself so that you can see what is important to you. Only then can you take control of your emotions and start making changes to your life. The better you are tuned in to how you feel, the better placed you will be to anticipate how you will respond to future events or interactions with others.

As mentioned in the introduction, we are generally more in touch with our thoughts than our feelings. As a consequence, we may be unaware of the extent to which we are emotionally driven. It's important to recognize that emotions always serve a purpose. By understanding the basics of why we feel the way we do, we make it easier for ourselves to process our emotions accurately. It's therefore worth dipping into the neuroscience here to explain the connection between emotions and our decision-making process. Emotions don't just stem from the heart – they are mental states brought on by neurophysiological changes. The control centre of our emotions is the limbic system of the brain: the hypothalamus, which controls our emotional responses; the amygdala (the trigger point of emotion); the hippocampus, which helps us preserve and retrieve memories; and the limbic cortex, which impacts our mood, motivation and judgement. Messages are transmitted to the brain by neurons via the spinal cord through the limbic cortex to the front of the brain, where we think rationally. This two-way flow of information travels constantly between the emotional and rational parts of the brain, which explains why emotions are integral to our decision-making process and behaviour. In highly emotionally intelligent people, this flow of information runs smoothly ,as they have a heightened awareness of their feelings and the impact those emotions have on their behaviour.

To gain greater self-knowledge, you need to adopt the role of a detective and take the time to identify your emotions. You then need to understand what causes these feelings and monitor your reaction to them both physically and mentally. For example, when you are feeling under pressure, you many experience the physical signs of stress such as knots in your stomach, a dry mouth and sweaty palms, whereas mentally you may feel out of control and anxious. Feelings of excitement can cause you to have butterflies in your tummy, a smile on your face and raised energy levels. One of the challenges of identifying your emotions is finding the language to accurately describe a diverse range of feelings. Emotions are often nuanced and finding the right word to articulate them can be tricky. A good example of this is the use of the term 'sadness.' Depending on your personal make-up and the situation, you could be feeling depressed, nostalgic, mournful or heartbroken. It's about finding a vocabulary of emotions that works for you. A useful tool to help you identify your feelings is the Plutchik Emotion Wheel.[8]

THE PLUTCHIK EMOTION WHEEL

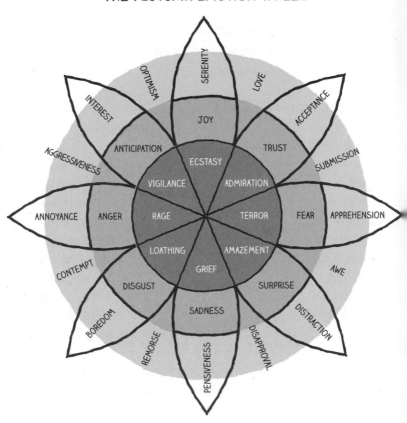

Psychologist Robert Plutchik created the wheel to help people identify, clarify and label complex emotions. The wheel shows four pairs of opposing emotions: joy and sadness, fear and anger, anticipation and surprise and disgust and trust. These basic emotions make up the first circle; the centre of the circle shows the more intense version of these feelings; the outer circle, the less intense version of them. The power of this wheel is showing how different emotions relate to one another and can intensify over time. For example contempt is a combination of annoyance and boredom, submission is midway between acceptance and apprehension. Referring to this wheel can help you recognize and verbalize the different emotions you experience on a daily basis.

KEY TAKEAWAYS

- Self-knowledge is your ability to recognize and understand your emotions and how they influence your judgement, decision-making and behaviour.
- Knowing yourself is not a one-off event – it's a conscious decision to become more self-aware.
- Self-knowledge helps you identify your strengths and limitations so you can adopt a growth mindset.
- The more tuned in you are to your emotions, the greater your sense of well-being.
- Emotions are mental states brought on by neurophysiological changes.
- Feelings and emotions are integral to our decision-making process.
- Use the Plutchik Emotion Wheel to help you label and articulate complex feelings.

2. UNDERSTANDING WHAT MAKES YOU TICK

Uncovering the real 'you' is crucial for your sense of well-being as well as your ability to build relationships with others. The more aware we are of how we feel, the easier it will be to manage these feelings and influence others. When we're younger, we tend to build our identity through the reactions of our family, our teachers and our friends. It's often only as adults that we have the opportunity to reflect and build a more accurate understanding of ourselves. It can be helpful to recognize that we all have three selves:

- **Our public self:** the way we believe others expect us to behave (this is the most likely to change).
- **Our self under stress:** our instinctive behaviour under pressure (this is the least likely to change).
- **Our perceived self:** how we see ourselves and believe we deal with others most of the time (this can change gradually with time).

It is only by building a clearer picture of your perceived self that you can begin to develop your emotional intelligence.

The secret to understanding what really makes you tick is to carve out time for yourself each day to connect to your emotions. This is easier said than done given the fast pace of daily life. Try to avoid digital distractions. Mindfulness is a powerful technique that can help you connect with your inner self. It enables you to be present in the moment so you can pay real attention to yourself and your surroundings. By living life in a more mindful way, you will increase your awareness of your inner state and how you react to things. Keeping a journal is another tool that allows you to reflect on your emotions and process them through writing.

EXERCISE

Keep a journal for the week ahead. Each day, reflect on a meaningful situation where you have your emotions switched on. If possible, choose a high-stakes situation that really matters to you. Notice your state of mind and what exactly triggers any strong emotions. As you experience these feelings, pay attention to yourself. Ask yourself: How are you reacting? What is taking place in your body and mind? How does this affect what you say and what you do?

It takes courage to give yourself an honest appraisal and write down your thoughts and feelings accurately. A lot of people shy away from facing their own reality. Perhaps you are scared of what you may uncover – after all, as the author Aldous Huxley said, "If most of us remain ignorant of ourselves, it is because self-knowledge is painful and we prefer the pleasures of illusion."

It's important to recognize that how you see yourself will change in different situations and with different people. A useful technique to help you gain a clearer understanding of what makes you tick is to identify your personality type and communication preference. It will also give you visibility of the nonverbal cues you give to other people.

By and large, people are predictably different. DISC is a useful tool that can help you get insight into your personality type's strengths, limitations and communication preferences. The diagram below shows how DISC works – everyone falls somewhere along the axes of 'outgoing' to 'reserved' and 'task orientated' to 'people focused.' Outgoing people get their energy from others, are fast-paced and are networkers. Reserved people get their energy from within, are more introverted and are considered. People who are task orientated enjoy processes, planning and projects. People-orientated types enjoy relationships, language and sharing ideas. DISC helps you to pinpoint where you fall on these axes and gives a detailed understanding of your personality type.

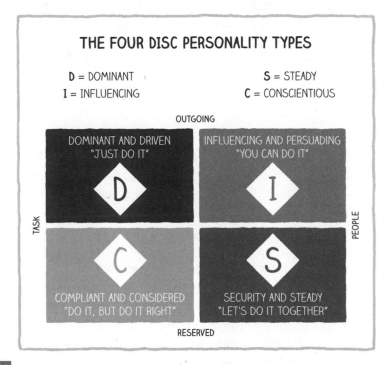

THE FOUR DISC PERSONALITY TYPES

D = DOMINANT
I = INFLUENCING

S = STEADY
C = CONSCIENTIOUS

OUTGOING

DOMINANT AND DRIVEN
"JUST DO IT"

D

INFLUENCING AND PERSUADING
"YOU CAN DO IT"

I

TASK

PEOPLE

C

COMPLIANT AND CONSIDERED
"DO IT, BUT DO IT RIGHT"

S

SECURITY AND STEADY
"LET'S DO IT TOGETHER"

RESERVED

A useful exercise to help you fully understand the DISC personality types is to imagine you're in a lift with a group of people. D types will purposely enter and immediately locate the button to close the doors; I types won't be able to resist making conversation with the other people; S types will be patiently holding the door open, saying there's plenty of room for more; and C types will be calculating the weight of everyone in the lift to make sure it doesn't exceed the maximum capacity! By recognizing your own personality type, you will become more informed about how you make decisions and understand how your personality type impacts others.

EXERCISE
Use the table below to help you identify your own personality type by choosing the comments that most closely align with your sense of yourself. Bear in mind that no one personality type is better than another and that usually you will be a blend of types.

DOMINANT (D)	INFLUENCING (I)	STEADY (S)	CONSCIENTIOUS (C)
I LIKE TO CHALLENGE MYSELF	I'M PERSUASIVE AND ENTHUSIASTIC	I'M CARING AND SUPPORTIVE OF OTHERS	I AM TASK FOCUSED AND HAVE STRONG ATTENTION TO DETAIL
I AM RESULTS DRIVEN	I PREFER TO FOCUS ON THE BIG PICTURE RATHER THAN GET BOGGED DOWN IN THE DETAILS	I'M A GOOD LISTENER	I AM ANALYTICAL AND ACCURATE

DOMINANT (D)	INFLUENCING (I)	STEADY (S)	CONSCIENTIOUS (C)
I AM HAPPY TO TAKE THE LEAD AND MAKE DECISIONS	I LIKE COLLABORATING AND SOCIALIZING AS A TEAM	I DON'T LIKE TO CHALLENGE THE STATUS QUO	I LIKE TO HAVE ALL THE INFORMATION AVAILABLE BEFORE I MAKE A DECISION
I AM COMPETITIVE	RELATIONSHIPS ARE IMPORTANT TO ME	FEELING APPRECIATED IS IMPORTANT TO ME	I PREFER WORKING INDEPENDENTLY
I WILL GET THE JOB DONE	I DON'T LIKE TO ROCK THE BOAT	I LIKE KEEPING THE PEACE	I DON'T LIKE SURPRISES

If you are a **D** personality type, you are motivated by power and authority, and your communication preference is to direct others and tell people what to do. You are fuelled by getting results. If you are an **I** personality type, you are motivated by praise and recognition, and your communication preference is to motivate and inspire others. You goal is to enjoy yourself. As an **S** personality type, you are motivated by security and harmony, and your communication preference is to listen. You like to preserve the status quo and put other people's needs before your own. Finally, if you are a **C** personality type, you are motivated by systems and procedures, and your communication preference is written. You value detail and accuracy.

Once you have identified your own personality type, it can be useful to imagine yourself on a good and bad day to help you build awareness of your strengths and limitations.

On a good day:
- **D types** are determined, focused and purposeful.
- **I types** are sociable, enthusiastic and persuasive.
- **S types** are caring, patient and amiable.
- **C types** are precise, questioning and analytical.

On a bad day:
- **D types** are controlling, aggressive and intolerant.
- **I types** are excitable, frantic and hasty.
- **S types** are bland, reliant and stubborn.
- **C types** are formal, suspicious and reserved.

Reflecting on your personality type in this way will help you gain a more accurate understanding of your impact on others. This will encourage you to evaluate how your self-image differs from what other people really think about you.

HOW TO IDENTIFY YOUR LEARNING STYLE

An important step in developing your self-knowledge is understanding what type of learner you are. Everyone processes information differently. It therefore helps if you can recognize your predominant learning style to make sure you learn in the most efficient way. Broadly speaking, there are four different learning styles:

- Visual learners
- Auditory learners
- Verbal learners
- Kinesthetic learners

Let's look at each of these learning styles in more detail. Visual learners prefer the use of images, such as maps and graphics, to help them process information. Auditory learners remember information by listening to podcasts and audiobooks and by actively speaking in seminars or workshops. Verbal learners rely on reading and writing to help them process new information. Finally, kinesthetic learners prefer to put the theory into practice by learning in a hands-on way, such as by following demonstration videos on YouTube or TikTok. By taking the time to understand your learning preference, you are helping to set yourself up for success by developing your emotional intelligence skills in the quickest and most efficient way.

To be able to learn effectively, we also need to be challenged. The Learning Zone diagram below, originally developed by Tom Senniger, shows the various zones we need to move through to develop as an individual and achieve true fulfilment in life.[9]

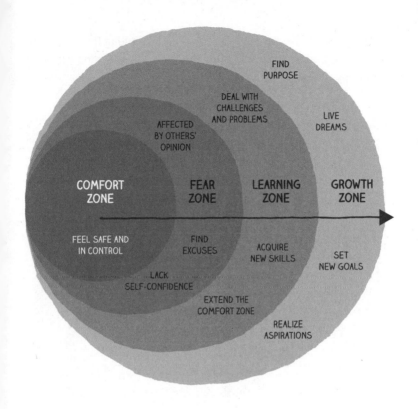

FIND
PURPOSE

DEAL WITH
CHALLENGES
AND PROBLEMS

LIVE
DREAMS

AFFECTED
BY OTHERS'
OPINION

**COMFORT
ZONE**

**FEAR
ZONE**

**LEARNING
ZONE**

**GROWTH
ZONE**

FEEL SAFE AND
IN CONTROL

FIND
EXCUSES

ACQUIRE
NEW SKILLS

SET
NEW GOALS

LACK
SELF-CONFIDENCE

EXTEND THE
COMFORT ZONE

REALIZE
ASPIRATIONS

The secret is to take the time to reflect on where you are at the current time. It can be easy to get stuck in your Comfort Zone, where you feel safe and secure, without even recognizing it. It's only by facing your fears and moving into your Learning Zone that you can really begin to grow. This is crucial for developing your emotional intelligence, as it holds the key to learning new skills. What zone you are in will vary depending on the situations you find yourself in on a daily basis. For example, you may be in your Comfort Zone at work, in a job you have done for years, and in your Fear Zone in a personal relationship that has only just begun (or vice versa). The key is to identify any self-limiting beliefs in your Fear Zone that may be holding you back and preventing you from achieving your full potential in your Growth Zone.

KEY TAKEAWAYS

- Be aware of your three selves: your public self, yourself under stress and your perceived self.
- Actively carve out time each day to connect with your emotions, using mindfulness and journaling to help you.
- Use DISC to help you identify your personality type and communication preference.
- Imagine yourself on a good and bad day to help you build awareness of your strengths and limitations.
- Identify your learning style so you can develop your emotional intelligence in the quickest and most efficient way.

3. UNCOVERING YOUR BLIND SPOTS

As a rule, it is easier to spot low levels of emotional intelligence in other people than it is in ourselves. One of the biggest barriers to truly knowing yourself are the blind spots and unconscious bias that mark the difference between how we see ourselves and how other people perceive us. The older and more experienced we become, the more likely we are to overestimate or underestimate our skills and strengths. This could be because we have fewer people who are prepared to give us honest feedback. It could also be because we are more likely to ask for feedback from people we get along with, rather than those we don't. A practical tool to help you uncover any blind spots is the Johari Window, a personal development technique created by a team of psychologists in the 1950s.[10]

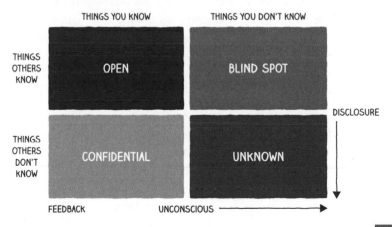

Let's start by looking at the window from your perspective:

- The **Open** box shows what both you and others know – this could be your level of technical expertise or strengths you are particularly proud of.
- The **Blind Spot** is what others know but you do not – perhaps you don't always understand the impact you have on others.
- The **Unknown** box is what neither you nor others know – this could be your full potential, for example if you haven't yet been fully tested or given the opportunity to be the best that you can be.
- The **Hidden** box is what you know but others do not – this can be where self-doubt and impostor syndrome lurk (self-limiting beliefs about your ability that you are reluctant to share with others).

If we now think of the Johari Window in the context of the Learning Zone model above, you can see that the Open window is closely linked to your Comfort Zone, the Hidden window relates to your Fear Zone and the Unknown window is your Growth Zone, where your true potential lies. It's only by moving into your Learning Zone that you (and those around you) will understand what is in your Unknown window and what you are truly capable of achieving.

EXERCISE

Start by selecting five to ten words to describe yourself. Then ask four trusted friends or colleagues to write down five to ten words that they think best describe you. By comparing your findings with those of your trusted friends or colleagues, you should be able to fill in your own Johari Window in the relevant sections below. This will help you increase your self-knowledge by closing down your blind spots so that you can build a more accurate picture of yourself.

	KNOWN TO SELF	UNKNOWN TO SELF
KNOWN TO OTHERS	OPEN	BLIND
UNKNOWN TO OTHERS	HIDDEN	UNKNOWN

Your goal should be to keep asking for feedback to help you add information to the Open box so that your self-knowledge increases and your Hidden and Unknown boxes get smaller.

MANAGING YOUR UNCONSCIOUS BIAS

One of the most common types of blind spots people experience is unconscious bias. Whether we like it or not, human beings are hardwired to make snap judgements. The human brain instinctively categorizes people to make sense of the world. In social interactions, people process information via two routes: one is automatic and the other is controlled. The automatic route is largely driven by emotional factors and activates well-established stereotypes. Our automatic social processing happens so quickly that it is below our level of consciousness, taking well below 100 milliseconds and potentially as little as 30 milliseconds.[11] It can influence our immediate judgements and behaviours without us even knowing it. This unconscious bias can be based on appearance, age, gender, skin colour and markers of social status, to name but a few. These deeply ingrained preconceptions and prejudices, formed from our upbringing and experiences, can affect our behaviour and lead to discrimination.

Although it is almost impossible to eliminate unconscious bias, we can override our reflexive responses with controlled and deliberate thought and reflection. This prevents our unconscious bias unknowingly influencing our behaviour and decision-making. You can do this by acknowledging your unconscious biases, becoming aware of how they impact your choices and behaviour towards others, and then making a choice to be different. Self-awareness is the key to this.

EXERCISE

Start by accepting that almost everyone has unconscious bias, then ask yourself what yours may be. What assumptions have you made about other people without a second thought? What has influenced your decision-making? How do you react to different types of people? Be brave and dig deep – it can be uncomfortable at first. It's only by taking the time to know yourself and recognize your own unconscious bias that you can begin to change your behaviour.

KEY TAKEAWAYS

- The biggest barriers to self-knowledge are blind spots and unconscious bias.
- Use the Johari Window to increase your self-knowledge and close down your blind spots.
- Accept that everyone has unconscious bias, then take steps to understand what yours might be by reflecting on how you react to different types of people and situations.
- Your aim is to override these reflexive responses with controlled and deliberate thought and reflection.

4. RECOGNIZING YOUR IMPACT ON OTHERS

Now that you have identified your personality type and how to override your unconscious bias, it's time to use the information you have gathered so far to understand the impact you have on other people. Self-knowledge is not just about introspection – while we need it to hold up a mirror to see ourselves, it's equally important to discover how other people see us. People want to know who they are dealing with. Being genuine and authentic holds the key to building trust and rapport. We feel more comfortable with people who show their true selves, rather than with people who hide behind a façade or image. If you are too guarded or difficult to read, people won't feel they can be themselves with you.

If you don't truly know yourself and manage your mood, you are more likely to misfire when it comes to landing your messages with others. This doesn't mean you should be striving for perfection – I believe we are all wonderfully flawed individuals. Rather, it's about communicating the real you. By displaying vulnerability, you will create a safe environment that encourages other people to lower their defences and share their thoughts and ideas. Remember, what you feel, say and do are inextricably linked. According to psychologist Albert Mehrabian, only 7% of communication comes from the actual words we use – 38% comes from our tone of voice and 55% comes from our body language and facial expressions.[12] You therefore need to take practical steps to showcase your emotional intelligence through what you say, how you say it and your nonverbal communication. You need to be consistent in how your land your messages whenever and however you interact with others. Whether you are communicating face to face, via email or over the phone, your goal should be to present the real you at every touchpoint. It can destroy trust if the person who is warm and engaging in person is abrupt and dismissive via email.

EXERCISE

A powerful way to recognize your impact on others is to ask for feedback on a regular basis. Refer back to the Johari Window and think carefully about who you want to receive feedback from. Ideally it should be a critic who is close to you or someone you trust who isn't afraid to tell you the truth. Consider the timing and be specific about what you are asking for. It is often easier to give feedback than it is to receive it, so here are some top tips to help you get the most out of the process:

- Keep an open mind to maximize the impact of what the other person has to say.
- Try to be grateful for the time and effort the other person has taken to give you constructive feedback.
- Listen attentively to what they have to say and above all avoid being defensive, argumentative or dismissive.
- Give yourself some time to digest their key points before responding, then ask questions to clarify anything you are unsure about.
- Many people find receiving feedback difficult, but it can be helpful to keep your strengths and talents front of mind to maintain a sense of perspective.
- Remind yourself of the positive intent behind the feedback – your goal should be to learn more about yourself in order to boost your performance and improve your relationships with those around you.

It's important to recognize that your personality type will have a direct impact on how you respond to feedback. Think back to the DISC model and use the following information to help you understand how you are most likely to react:

- If you are a **D** personality type, you are generally open to feedback but will want the other person to get to the point straightaway. You will want to have your voice heard and may be direct in your response. You will quickly put an action plan in place to 'fix' any issues.

- If you are an **I** personality type, you like to be praised so can find receiving feedback particularly challenging. You are more likely to respond emotionally. You therefore need to take time to process your feelings so you can take the feedback on board. You may find it hard to agree on next steps and put a plan in place.

- If you are an **S** personality type, you can find feedback unsettling and will want to receive detailed examples to understand it. You may need to review the feedback with other people before you can fully accept it. You are also likely to want to follow up with the person giving the feedback at a later date.

- If you are a **C** personality type, you will want to see concrete evidence to back up the feedback. You will expect any feedback to be accurate and will struggle to accept vague comments. You may find it difficult to open up with the other person and are likely to hide any emotion.

Whatever your personality type, once you have received the feedback, you need to take steps to change your behaviour so that you can take your emotional intelligence to the next level. This can be easier said than done. Remember – it's a strength to ask for help. It can be useful to find a coach or therapist to provide support and hold you to account as you make these changes.

People often mistakenly see self-reflection as self-indulgent, when in fact it's crucial to helping you lead a more successful life. It's only by understanding your strengths and areas for development that you can keep learning and growing. Don't be disheartened if, after your initial appraisal, you're not where you want to be. All too often our confidence is rooted in *what* we do, when in fact we should be focusing on *how* we do things. This requires a change in mindset. None of us is the finished article – we all have imperfections. It's about putting in the time and effort to be the best that we can be. Self-knowledge on its own is not enough. It's now up to you to do the work and build on this foundation by making a plan to improve your other emotional intelligence skills.

KEY TAKEAWAYS

- A key part of self-knowledge is understanding the impact you have on other people.
- Highly emotionally intelligent people communicate their true selves in order to build trust and rapport.
- You need to communicate the real you at all touchpoints: whether in person, via email or on the phone.
- Ask for feedback from loving critics to help you understand how other people perceive you.
- Focus on *how* you do things, instead of *what* you do, to take your emotional intelligence to the next level.
- Don't strive for perfection – commit to putting in the time and effort to becoming the best version of yourself.

PART TWO

MANAGING
YOURSELF

Once you have done the hard work of getting to know yourself better, the next step on your journey to leading a more successful life is to learn how to manage your emotions in a more productive way. If we refer back to our definition of emotional intelligence as **the ability to recognize and manage your own emotions and those of others**, it's clear that successful people use their self-knowledge to help them control impulsive feelings so they can think rationally and achieve their goals.

Self-management is critical to success in life, as it allows you to stay cool, calm and collected in stressful situations. Developing your self-management skills will increase your clarity of thought and ability to make effective decisions. Whether it's managing your frustration, controlling your anger or facing up to your lack of confidence, learning how to regulate these feelings will help you execute your goals and withstand the pressures of daily life.

FIVE SIGNS YOU NEED TO DEVELOP YOUR SELF-MANAGEMENT SKILLS

- You procrastinate and put off the jobs you don't enjoy.
- You experience red mist and find it difficult to control your anger or frustration.
- You are easily distracted and find it difficult to stay focused on the task in hand.
- You lack willpower and struggle to achieve your goals.
- You experience self-doubt and have low self-esteem.

In order to become the best version of yourself, it's helpful to break down self-management into its three building blocks: self-control, self-reliance and self-confidence. You then need to use the knowledge you've gathered from developing your self-awareness to identify which areas need the most work. Your time and energy are limited. According to Parkinson's Law, the amount of work expands to fill the time available for its completion.[13] In other words, if you give yourself a week to finish a task, you are likely to fill up your time doing it. The secret to setting yourself up for success is focusing on the areas that need the most work. This way you'll avoid being a busy fool – spending too much time on things that don't really matter. It's about taking a conscious and disciplined approach to managing yourself.

Changing your behaviour is easy to say but hard to do. As a rule, what gets measured gets done. This is where a coach, mentor or trusted friend comes in – they can help to hold you to account as you develop your new skills. Developing your self-management skills won't happen overnight – you are in it for the long run. It's about setting short-, medium- and long-term goals to help you control your emotions, back yourself and boost your confidence. It's only by following the practical steps below that you will learn how to be fully accountable for your thoughts, actions and behaviours.

1. CONTROLLING YOUR EMOTIONS

When people think about emotional intelligence, they often focus on empathy and social skills and undervalue the critical role self-control plays in helping them to live a successful life. Many people are more likely to notice a lack of self-control in others than in themselves. On the one end of the spectrum, and perhaps easier to spot, are people losing their temper or behaving unreasonably in the workplace. On the other end of the spectrum, and perhaps harder to pick up, is someone suffering with crippling nerves or struggling to meet deadlines. It will come as no surprise that experiencing these heightened emotions can reduce our ability to think logically. Whatever the underlying cause, we all need self-control to calm our minds so that we can make rational and balanced decisions. People with high levels of self-control are seen as a safe pair of hands. They have the discipline and willpower to achieve their goals ,although it's worth noting that too much self-control can lead to controlling behaviour. It can also make you appear detached and cold as you try too hard to control every aspect of your behaviour.

The first step in learning to manage yourself more effectively is to focus your attention on what you can control, not what you can't. We are not responsible for everything that happens around us so try to avoid spending a lot of time and energy worrying about things you cannot change. Your goal should be to control the controllables.

A useful tool to help you manage yourself more productively is the Circles of Control, shown in the diagram below.

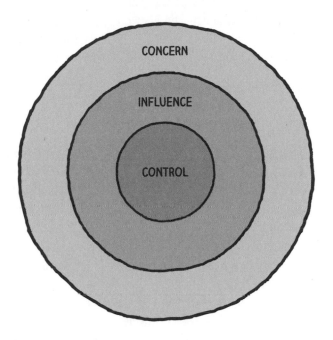

The inner circle represents the things that are for the most part within your control, such as where you live, the work you do, your attitude to life, what you read and the words you use. The middle circle is your area of influence – those things that you can still do something about, such as the quality of your work, the relationships you form and the results you achieve. The outer circle is your area of concern and it contains things over which you have no control, such as the traffic, terrorism, a global pandemic, foreign policy or natural disasters – events that you can spend a lot of time agonizing over but that ultimately you are powerless to change. Your aim should be to consciously focus your attention on those things within your Control and Influence circles – things that you can actually do something about – and not burn your energy on factors outside your control. I certainly felt that, in the early part of the global Covid-19 pandemic, the virus had invaded my zone of control. I had to work very hard to push it back out to my zone of concern.

Unfortunately, our ability to focus is constantly challenged by new technology. We are more distracted than ever before. According to a study from researchers at Harvard University, people spend 47% of their waking hours distracted, thinking about something other than what they are doing.[14] This is echoed by research finding that our attention span has markedly decreased in recent years. In 2000 it was 12 seconds, whereas 15 years later it had shrunk significantly to 8.25 seconds.[15] Given the scale of the challenge, it clearly takes great self-control to keep your eye on the ball and stay focused and present on tasks and conversations. If you recognize that you are easily distracted, the great news is that there are mental exercises you can do to strengthen your brain circuitry to improve your attention. In his book *Focus: The Hidden Driver of Excellence*, Daniel Goleman describes attention as like a muscle – the more you practise using it, the stronger it will become.[16]

The following mindfulness techniques may be helpful in developing your cognitive ability by improving your attention span and encouraging you to focus on the present. They are about being aware of when your mind drifts and consciously bringing it back to the here and now.

It's only by learning how to be truly present in the moment that you can make the best use of the time available to you. As business guru Michael Altshuler is widely reputed to have said, "The bad news is that time flies. The good news is that you're the pilot." Self-control is key to helping you manage your time effectively. As humans, we constantly look for shortcuts or the easy option. It can be very tempting to procrastinate and put off those jobs you dislike doing or find the most challenging. Common reasons why we procrastinate include fear of failure, perfectionism, lack of confidence and disinterest. Our day-to-day lives are packed with time-stealers that prevent us from ticking off our to-do list. Examples include back-to-back meetings, replying to emails 24/7 and constantly checking your phone. The secret to breaking this cycle is to harness your self-control so you can work smarter, not harder.

My BREAKS acronym can help you break the cycle of procrastination:
- **B**ite-size chunks: you don't have to complete a task in one go – break it down into manageable steps.
- **R**emove distractions and barriers: limit the time spent checking your phone or emails, or surfing the Web.
- **E**arly start: 'eat the frog' and do your most challenging task first when you have the most energy.
- **A**sk for help: you don't have to do everything on your own – don't be afraid to reach out for support.
- **K**eep motivated with rewards: incentivize your good behaviour by rewarding yourself when you've completed your tasks.
- **S**et deadlines: hold yourself to account by giving yourself a timeline.

Complete the exercise below to help you understand how you can use these techniques on a daily basis to keep you on track.

EXERCISE

Think about what's on your to-do list for the week ahead to help you identify those things you are procrastinating about. Then draw on your self-control to plan how you will take action to fix this. Root your action in time and place to help hold yourself to account.

WHAT I'M PROCRASTINATING OVER	MY COMMITMENT TO TAKING ACTION (WHAT? WHEN? HOW?)

THE FOUR Ds TOOL

Another tool that can help you manage your time more effectively so you can achieve a better work-life balance is the Four Ds of Time Management: Do, Delay, Drop and Delegate.[17]

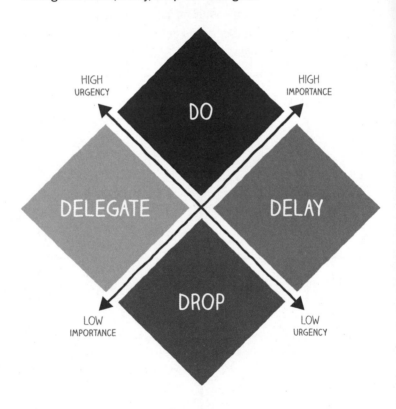

Deciding which tasks to do, delay, drop or delegate – depending on their level of urgency – will help to boost your productivity and keep you focused on achieving your end goal. You are far more likely to stay focused on what really matters to you if you prioritize instead of procrastinate by following the steps below:

DO IT

You've got a to-do list as long as your arm and you're called into a meeting about an urgent problem with your key client. The choice is clear – prioritize this issue immediately so you can try to resolve it as soon as possible. You won't even have the chance to procrastinate, as the sense of urgency will spur you into action. The same rule is true of all urgent, highly important tasks: they should be prioritized and put at the top of your list.

DELAY IT

It's impossible to do everything immediately, so it's essential to prioritize your workload in a logical and time-efficient manner. For tasks that are important but not urgent, the best advice is to delay them until you have dealt with more pressing issues. However, it's essential to remember that these are still important tasks that cannot be forgotten, so make sure you carve out time to deal with them effectively at a later date.

DROP IT

Whether it's an email you've been meaning to reply to since 2022 or some research you keep hoping to do, we all have tasks on our to-do list that we should actually get rid of. I'm talking about those unimportant, low-urgency jobs that eat up our time and don't add any real value. Forget them – erase them from your list and you will immediately feel more liberated. By prioritizing in this way, you will have more time to focus on the important tasks at hand and not get distracted by time wasters.

DELEGATE IT

Mastering the art of delegation is crucial to working efficiently. No one can do everything. Therefore, when you're managing your workload, consider which of the urgent but low-importance tasks can be delegated to others. The key to delegating successfully is choosing the right person and explaining clearly and precisely what you expect them to do. Remember to encourage a real sense of ownership while allowing them enough time to complete the task.

———

Having the self-control to assess each task on your to-do list in this way will help you adopt a more productive way of working that will set you up for success in life. It's worth noting that people generally find it easier to complete tasks in their Do It list because the other three categories often require a conversation with another person, which can mean having less control over the outcome. So, try to challenge yourself to take the appropriate action, not necessarily the easiest one.

KEY TAKEAWAYS

- Managing yourself is about using your self-knowledge to control your emotions so you can think rationally and achieve your goals.
- Self-management consists of three building blocks: self-control, self-reliance and self-confidence.
- Focus your energy on the areas that need the most work to maximize the time available to you for self-development.
- Control the controllables and work on those things you can change, rather than those you can't.
- Use mindfulness techniques to help improve your attention span so you can avoid distractions and stay focused on the task at hand.
- BREAK the cycle of procrastination so you can work smarter, not harder.
- Apply the Four Ds – Do, Delay, Drop and Delegate – to manage your time better and achieve a better work-life balance.

2. MANAGING YOUR BEHAVIOUR

Once you have prioritized exactly what you want to work on, it's helpful to think about the role you adopt in emotionally charged situations so you can start to control your behaviour. The Drama Triangle, first described by psychologist Stephen Karpman in 1968, shows the three roles we consciously or unconsciously fall into in stressful or high conflict situations.[18]

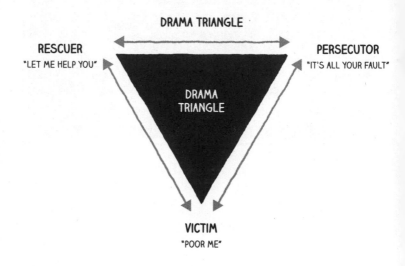

DRAMA TRIANGLE

RESCUER
"LET ME HELP YOU"

DRAMA TRIANGLE

PERSECUTOR
"IT'S ALL YOUR FAULT"

VICTIM
"POOR ME"

Are you a Victim, a Rescuer or a Persecutor? It's important to identify which role you tend to play so that you can break out of the trap and take control of the situation. If we look at each of the roles in turn, we can see that the **Victim** feels helpless and downtrodden. They don't believe they have the power to change the situation they are in and instead tend to wallow in self-pity. They are likely to blame the Persecutor for all their problems and look to the Rescuer for help. The **Rescuer** constantly tries to help others. They put other people's needs before their own and can feel stressed and tired as a result. Their actions can mean the Victim remains dependent on them. The **Persecutor** is often critical and controlling. They tend to blame the Victim and criticize the actions of the Rescuer. They constantly find fault and can sometimes resort to bullying behaviour. It's important to recognize that the role you play can change depending on the dynamics of the situation and the personalities of the people involved. To escape the Drama Triangle, you need to draw on your self-control to take action and change your behaviour. You goal should be to shift the dynamics, so you transition from Victim to Survivor, Persecutor to Challenger and Rescuer to Coach.

To understand how this can play out in real life, let's use the example of a performance review where an individual receives poor feedback. In this scenario, the Victim is the recipient of the feedback, who feels their performance is being judged unfairly and harshly. The Persecutor is the manager whose responsibility it is to deliver the difficult message. The Rescuer is an HR professional – the person the Victim turns to in their hour of need and asks to defend their performance. Shifting the dynamics requires the Victim to adopt an open mindset, take on board the feedback and take action to improve their performance so they can transition to become a Survivor. The manager must deliver the feedback in a meaningful way and flex their communication style so that the review is seen as constructive rather than critical. This way, they will shift their role from Persecutor to Challenger, where they are challenging the recipient of the feedback to be the best that they can be. Finally, the HR professional needs to take steps to support the Victim as they improve their performance – perhaps by providing access to training or to a mentor. By helping the Victim find their own way forward, they are transitioning from Rescuer to Coach.

The secret to changing your behaviour is learning how to manage your state when your emotions are triggered. As discussed in Part One, an emotional trigger is something that provokes a strong emotional reaction to a particular individual, situation or dialogue. In its most extreme form, it can cause a flight, freeze or fight response. Once you are triggered in this way, it is difficult to stay calm, think effectively and find a new way forward. Refer back to page 27 and use the knowledge you have gathered about your various triggers to understand how best to control them. Remember, triggers come from many origins – they might include your manager, work pressures, change, performance expectations or your own expectations of yourself.

EXERCISE

A powerful coaching technique to help you manage your emotional triggers and retrain your brain is to ask yourself the following three questions:

- What will happen if I react to my trigger?
- What won't happen if I react to my trigger?
- What will happen if I don't react to my trigger?

Perhaps you are triggered by other people challenging your ideas. If you react, you are likely to act defensively and fight back. This could mean you ignore the other person's ideas, which could damage your relationship with them. If you don't react to your trigger, you are more likely to listen to what the other person has to say and work collaboratively to find a solution that works for both parties.

This all sounds very reasonable and logical. However, thinking on your feet and managing triggers live in the moment can be difficult. This is because you are trying to control an instinctive and deeply ingrained reaction. Here are some top tips to help you draw on your self-control so you have the bandwidth to respond rather than react to emotional situations:

- Don't respond immediately
- Take a deep breath and steady yourself
- Remind yourself that this feeling is temporary
- Focus on the bigger picture
- Find a healthy outlet
- Take a break or get some fresh air

- Try to depersonalize the situation
- Don't sweat the small stuff

A good way to understand how to keep your emotions in check is to reflect on what pilots do in an emergency. They control their fight, freeze or flight response to a crisis by following the 'Aviate, Navigate and Communicate' rule.[19] In other words, the priority is to keep flying the plane, the next step is to find an emergency landing spot and only when the situation is under control does the pilot communicate to the passengers. Adopting this disciplined approach allows their mind to work in a rational way. A great way to embed these habits and behaviours is to adopt the principle of Plan, Do and Review by following the actions below:

- **Plan:** Anticipate any curve balls that might come your way and prepare how you would like to respond.
- **Do:** Follow the bullet points above to help control your behaviour so you respond rather than react to those situations or people.
- **Review:** Take the time to reflect on how this went – ask yourself what worked well and what you would do differently next time.

By recognizing your triggers, reflecting on the impact they have on you and other people, and responding with control, you will learn how to be truly accountable for your behaviour.

KEY TAKEAWAYS

- Understand the behaviour you exhibit in emotionally charged situations by referring to the Drama Triangle.
- Ask yourself whether you tend to be a Victim, Rescuer or Persecutor.
- Take action to manage your state so you can retrain your brain and change your behaviour.
- Learn to keep your emotions in check by applying the rule of Plan, Do and Review.

3. LEARNING TO BACK YOURSELF

The next step in developing your self-management is learning how to become more self-reliant. This is about being accountable for your thoughts and emotions and taking responsibility for your actions and behaviour. People with high levels of self-reliance have the self-assurance and initiative to develop their own ideas, rise to new challenges and make independent decisions. They have the confidence to direct others and take charge in challenging situations. People with low levels of self-reliance, on the other hand, tend to hide behind others. This can make them appear subservient and seem to be people pleasers (which is different from being focused on others). As a rule, they defer to other people's opinions rather than having the confidence to voice their own perspective. In a worst-case scenario, they can end up being taken advantage of or bullied. Nelson Mandela displayed exceptional levels of self-reliance when, after 27 years imprisoned on Robben Island and elsewhere, he had the strength of character to forgive his captors and the self-reliance to continue his fight. Mandela famously found strength in this quote from the poem "Invictus" by William Ernest Henley: "I am the master of my fate, I am the captain of my soul."[20] It is this belief that you can steer your own course in life that lies at the very heart of self-reliance.

As children we look to parents, teachers or adults for guidance and advice when it comes to making decisions. For some people this pattern of codependency continues into adulthood – they rely on their partner, a colleague or their boss for help instead of taking matters into their own hands. The secret to developing your self-reliance is to overcome those barriers that prevent you from making independent decisions. Common examples include the fear of failure or rejection, insecurities about your ability, and concerns over what other people think of you. These barriers can paralyse your decision-making so that you constantly look to others for affirmation and reassurance. You therefore need to take the time to identify the specific barriers that prevent you from developing your self-reliance. The Five Whys, developed by Taiichi Ohno, is a very simple brainstorming tool that will help you delve deeper and understand the root cause of the problems you are facing.[21]

EXERCISE

Find out what is holding you back when it comes to independent decision-making, by asking yourself "why?" five times to help you drill down and get to the root cause of the problem.

THE 5 WHYS

DEFINE THE PROBLEM

WHY IS IT HAPPENING?

WHY IS THAT?

WHY IS THAT?

WHY IS THAT?

WHY IS THAT?

ROOT CAUSE

An example could be:

- **Problem:** I find it difficult to say no.
- **Why is it happening?** People in the team are taking advantage of my goodwill.
- **Why is that?** I don't like confrontation.
- **Why is that?** I don't feel confident enough to voice my own opinion.
- **Why is that?** I worry that I will say the wrong thing.
- **Why is that?** I care too much what other people think about me.
- **Root cause:** The desire to please is undermining your self-reliance.

Once you have identified the root cause, you need to evaluate whether this is something you can live with, in which case you need to let it go and let the emotional baggage go with it. If it's something you need to work on, then you need to put an action plan in place to help you. The way to start is by changing your mindset and transitioning from Victim to Survivor. For, as Eleanor Roosevelt is widely quoted as having said, "No one can make you feel inferior without your consent." It's about setting new goals so you can be true to yourself and have the confidence to find your own way.

EXERCISE

Fill in the boxes below to help you prioritize the steps you need to take to become more self-assured. The first row has been filled in using the previous example of someone who struggles to say no to the people in their team.

START	STOP	CONTINUE
VOICING YOUR OPINION IN THE NEXT TEAM MEETING	AGREEING WITH EVERYONE TO MAINTAIN THE STATUS QUO	THINKING CREATIVELY AND SOLVING PROBLEMS

As you take these steps, you need to be prepared for things to go wrong from time to time. If situations don't turn out like you planned, remember to take the learnings and move on. As you begin to make more independent decisions, you should expect to be challenged. You therefore need to leverage your resilience so that this doesn't knock your confidence. It's about having the courage of your convictions while being prepared to own your mistakes. The more you do this, the more confident you will be to back yourself in a range of situations.

One final word of caution: avoid taking your self-reliance too far. No one is an island and everything has consequences. Don't be afraid to lean on others when the situation calls for it – for example, if you need specific information or a consensus in order to reach a decision. It's important to differentiate between being self-reliant and being stubborn or autocratic. You should aim to use your judgement to be appropriately self-assured.

KEY TAKEAWAYS

- Self-reliance is about backing yourself and being accountable for your decisions and actions.
- People with high levels of self-reliance take the initiative and steer their own course in life.
- A lack of self-reliance can lead to submission and subservience, which can limit your ability to lead a successful life.
- Use the Five Whys tool to identify any barriers that are preventing you from making independent decisions.
- Once you have identified the root cause of the problem, draw up an action plan to solve it using the Start, Stop and Continue coaching technique.

4. BOOSTING YOUR SELF-CONFIDENCE

There is clearly a strong relationship between self-reliance and self-confidence. In order to truly back yourself, you need to have confidence in your own abilities. People with high levels of self-confidence are comfortable in their own skin and like themselves. This confidence in their skills, judgement and abilities gives them the impetus they need to achieve their goals. If you feel good about yourself, you are more likely to have the motivation to achieve your full potential. It's about valuing who you are, what you do and what you have.

It's important to recognize that confidence can be both overplayed and underplayed. Too much confidence can come across as arrogance or aggression, whereas underplayed confidence can be seen as submission or subservience. In both cases, this will affect how you build relationships with others. If you behave in a subservient way, people in general and even the nicest, kindest people are likely to take advantage of you. If, on the other hand, you are arrogant, people will want to take you down a peg or two. It's about being appropriately confident. In life, people buy people. If you don't believe in yourself, you will be hard pressed to convince others to believe in you too. This is true whether you are trying to 'sell' yourself in an interview, persuade a customer to buy your product or influence people in your team to buy in to your idea. A lack of self-confidence will put you on the back foot in each scenario.

It can lead to self-doubt and low self-esteem, which can limit your success in life.

If you do suffer from a lack of self-confidence, you are certainly not alone. A surprisingly large number of high achievers suffer from impostor syndrome – "feelings of inadequacy that persist despite evident success."[22] Almost 70% of us feel like a fraud at one time or another during our lifetime.[23] Meryl Streep revealed her lack of confidence when she said, "You think, why would anyone want to see me again in a movie? And I don't know how to act anyway, so why am I doing this?"[24] Michelle Obama was equally candid in an interview when she said, "I still have a little impostor syndrome. It doesn't go away, that feeling that you shouldn't take me that seriously. What do I know? I share that with you because we all have doubts in our abilities, about our power and what that power is."[25]

This self-doubt can affect our ability to perform. We are often our own worst enemy, talking ourselves out of opportunities before we've even begun. The secret to banishing impostor syndrome is to silence that negative voice inside your head that tells you why you can't achieve something. You need to remind yourself, instead, of what's great about you, your work and your relationships with your friends, family and colleagues. By focusing on your strengths and achievements, you will reap the rewards of increased confidence and improved performance.

It's entirely normal to feel out of your depth from time to time. The key to boosting your confidence is to set new goals and achieve them. However, when your self-esteem takes a tumble, it can be even harder to move out of your Comfort Zone (see Part One). It's called a Comfort Zone for a reason – it's the place where you feel safe and secure. It can also lead to negative emotions, as it can cause you to shy away from new opportunities. It is only by pushing your limits and moving into your Learning Zone that you will develop as an individual and boost your self-confidence. So, face your fears and write a list of your main concerns and worries, such as "They're never going to promote me." Then think of a way to overcome this, such as asking yourself, "What are the skill gaps I need to close to put myself in the best position to be promoted?"

The next step to help you achieve new goals is to visualize what success looks like – whether it's posting your new job title on LinkedIn or imagining signing your name on a contract with a customer. By picturing what good looks like, you are more likely to develop a winning mindset that will boost your self-belief. The more you do, the more you *can* do.

EXERCISE

Refer back to the Learning Zone diagram on page 33 and ask yourself the following questions. They will help you understand what you are truly capable of achieving so that you can become the best version of yourself:

How often am I in my Comfort Zone?

How would I know I'm in my Fear Zone?

_____

_____

What are my Learning Zone opportunities?

_____

_____

How would it feel to be in my Growth Zone?

_____

_____

What helps me to be my best self?

_____

_____

Although it's important to keep challenging yourself, avoid setting exceptionally high standards, as this can ultimately lead to disappointment and demotivation. Give yourself permission to make mistakes. Remind yourself that good is good enough and try not to judge yourself more harshly than you judge others. Thriving as an individual means looking after yourself. Think of what you would say to your best friend in a similar situation, then follow your own advice. Get on top of your fear and remind yourself that you can't be good at everything. After all, no one is perfect, so don't try to please people at all costs. People pleasers often mistakenly believe they need to 'fake it until they make it' to convince others of their expertise, when in fact the secret to success is having the confidence to connect with other people in a genuine way. It's about embracing your imperfections and showing other people that you have nothing to hide. Being true to yourself – and not just talking the talk – will help you build trust, making it easier for the other person to agree with your point of view. Don't confuse self-confidence with bravado. It's not about being the most outgoing person in the room – it's about having an inner confidence that helps to build likeability. A great example is Richard Branson's authentic style of leadership. There is no façade: his customers genuinely feel they are getting to know the real him and this helps him build trust in his brand.[26]

Having examined in detail the three building blocks that make up self-management – self-control, self-reliance and self-confidence – it is helpful to see how these skills interlink to boost your emotional intelligence. A powerful way to learn and embed new skills is to use other people's behaviour as a role model. There can be no greater role model than President Volodymyr Zelenskyy, who displays exceptionally high levels of emotional intelligence. Zelenskyy has shown impressive self-control and discipline as he has managed the unimaginable pressure of leading a country at war. He has kept his nerve, remaining steadfast in his commitment to defend Ukraine. His self-reliance was clear for everyone to see when he stated, "I need ammunition, not a ride" in response to the USA's offer to evacuate him at the start of the invasion.[27] Despite his having no previous military or political experience, Zelenskyy's confidence in his ability to lead has inspired his fellow Ukrainians to keep fighting for freedom. It is a lesson to all of us about the power of leading with integrity, communicating with authenticity and balancing confidence with humility. Thankfully most of us don't have the pressure of developing these skills on the world stage against an aggressor that threatens our very existence. The secret to honing your self-management skills is to start small with a low-risk situation. Once you've mastered an easy situation, you can pick something harder. By taking practical steps to manage yourself in front of a bigger audience, you will quickly see your self-control, self-reliance and self-confidence grow.

KEY TAKEAWAYS

- In order to back yourself, you need confidence in your skills, judgement and abilities.
- It's about being appropriately confident (neither arrogant nor subservient).
- Banish any feelings of impostor syndrome by focusing on what's great about you, the work you do and your relationships with others.
- Silence any self-doubt by facing your fears and visualizing what success looks like to you.
- Embrace your imperfections and feel comfortable in your own skin by valuing who are, what you do and what you have.
- Keep challenging yourself to move into your Learning Zone and reap the rewards of improved confidence and performance.
- Use role modelling to help you develop your self-control, self-reliance and self-confidence so you can embed these skills as part of your daily routine.

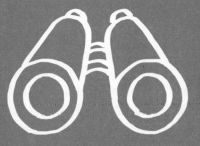

PART THREE

NAVIGATING THE WORLD AROUND YOU

In this part of the book, we are going to focus on the set of emotional intelligence skills that help you navigate the world around you. These are the core skills that give you a sense of perspective and future focus. They include ambition (your ability to set new goals), adaptability (your willingness to embrace change), optimism (your capacity to solve problems and adopt a positive outlook), work-life balance (your ability to balance your career with the things you enjoy) and self-actualization (your commitment to achieving your full potential).

As we know only too well, the world is full of uncertainty and change. We are inundated with news 24/7 reminding us how fragile and precarious life can be. Change is inevitable – in fact, it is the only constant in life. Rather than shy away from new challenges, people with high levels of emotional intelligence are able to deal with ambiguity and handle the unpredictable. They are brave and front-footed. This gives them the confidence to move out of their Comfort Zone, through their Fear Zone and into their Growth Zone (see page 33). It's about adopting a growth mindset and trying something new rather than sticking with the tried and tested. After all, in a quote famously attributed to Albert Einstein, "The definition of insanity is doing the same thing over and over again and expecting a different result." By equipping yourself with these key emotional intelligence skills, you will have the tools and techniques at your fingertips to plot your own course and achieve true fulfilment in life.

1. DIALLING UP YOUR AMBITION

The secret to becoming the best version of yourself is to set your sights high. Ambition holds the key to helping you reach new heights and achieve your goals. It boosts your energy levels and gives you the drive to succeed. I'm not talking about being ruthless and pursuing your goals at all costs – it's about cultivating a healthy level of ambition. People sometimes mistakenly see ambition as being synonymous with money and power, when, in fact, it depends on the aspirations of the individual. I often ask my clients what advice they would give their younger selves. More often than not, it's to have the courage of their convictions and go after what they want. Dialling up your ambition is about taking risks and challenging the status quo so you achieve the outcome you deserve.

I'm a big believer that if you don't ask, you don't get. Unfortunately, women are often less ambitious in their ask than their male counterparts. Whereas ambition is generally seen as an admirable trait in men, research shows that ambitious women are often criticized as being pushy or unlikeable. Sheryl Sandberg highlights this disparity in her book, *Lean In*, when she says, "Women don't take enough risks. Men are just 'foot on the gas pedal.' We're not going to close the achievement gap until we close the ambition gap."[28] Women are more likely to compromise on their goals and often negotiate with themselves, which can ultimately undermine their position. Unfortunately, too much stability can lead to missed opportunities and mediocrity. It's about identifying what success means to you and setting ambitious goals that keep you moving forward. A great role model is Michelle Obama, who was told by a career counsellor at school that she wasn't "Princeton material." Instead of lowering her expectations, she dialled up her ambition to successfully prove her counsellor wrong.[29]

It's time to follow Michelle Obama's example and start as you mean to go on by drawing on your ambition to set short-, medium- and long-term goals. These goals should be specific, measurable, achieveable, realistic and time-bound (SMART). It's about adopting an optimistic approach that encourages you to seek out new opportunities. By making sure your SMART goals are both ambitious and achievable, you will create a momentum for change that will motivate you on your journey. By keeping your eyes focused on the end game, you'll have a clear understanding of what you need to achieve going forward so you can control your ultimate destination.

EXERCISE

Identify a goal you want to achieve and use the table below to write it down using positive language. Set yourself up for success by fixing your goal in time and place, ensuring it is both measurable and realistically achievable. An example of a SMART goal could be, "I want to develop my communication skills so I can deliver my presentation with 50% more confidence at the September conference."

S	M	A	R	T
SPECIFIC	MEASURABLE	ACHEIVABLE	REALISTIC	TIME-BOUND
SPECIAL	MANAGEABLE	ATTAINABLE	RELEVANT	TIMELY
SERIOUS	MOTIVATING	AMBITOUS	RIGHT THING	TRACKABLE
STEPPED	MEANINGFUL	ACTION-ORIENTATED	RESULTS-BASED	TESTABLE

All too often, people set themselves a vague goal that is hard to achieve, such as "I'd like to get a new job," or an overly ambitious one, such as "Next year, I'd like to be CEO." This can be demoralizing in the long run. A smarter goal would be, "I want to secure a new marketing job in the pharmaceutical industry that makes use of my experience and technical skills. It needs to be within an hour's commute from where I live and I want to land it within the next 12 months." By fixing your goal in time and place and being appropriately realistic, you are setting yourself up for success. The key is to write your goal down, using positive language, then hold yourself to account by asking someone to support you on your journey to achieving it to help you measure your success.

By asking yourself, "What are the most important things to achieve this week?" and then identifying your key priorities for the month, you are more likely to achieve your long-term goal. If we take the example of finding a new job, your short-term goal could be to update your LinkedIn profile and connect with at least a dozen meaningful new people by the end of the week, and your medium-term goal could be to complete an online digital marketing course to hone your marketing skills in the next three months. This will help you stand out from the competition and make it more likely that you will achieve your long-term goal of securing a new marketing role in 12 months' time. If, at any time, you feel your motivation levels are dipping, take a moment to reflect on the benefits and downsides of whether or not you achieve your long-term goal. Start by asking yourself what will happen if you achieve this goal. Your answer could be, "I will feel excited and motivated about the work I do." Then ask yourself what will happen if you don't achieve this goal – for example, "I will feel stuck in a rut and this will undermine my confidence in the long run." Finish by asking yourself what won't happen if you don't achieve this goal. An example could be, "I will be unlikely to put myself forward for other marketing roles." By looking at the pros and cons of achieving your goals in this way, you will feel renewed determination and willpower to keep raising the bar.

KEY TAKEAWAYS

- You need to develop your ambition, adaptability, optimism and self-actualization to gain a sense of perspective and future focus.
- Dial up your ambition to help you take risks and reach new heights so you can be the best version of yourself.
- Set short-, medium- and long-term goals to help motivate you on your journey.
- These goals should be specific, measurable, ambitious, realistic and time-bound.

2. EMBRACING CHANGE

Given the fast-paced nature of the world around us, it's never been more important to adapt to new situations and accept that change is an integral part of life. People with high levels of adaptability adjust easily to new situations, are open to other people's ideas and enjoy new challenges. Embracing change is hard. It's not surprising that it doesn't come naturally to everyone. People with low levels of adaptability prefer a predictable daily routine, find it difficult to change an opinion and like to stick with the tried and tested. Thankfully, as the Covid-19 pandemic showed us, most of us are more adaptable that we realize.

The curve change model shown below is a useful tool that can help you understand people's response to change. Based on a model developed in the 1960s by Elisabeth Kübler-Ross to explain the grieving process, the Change Curve shows the four emotional states people go through as they experience change: shock or denial, anger or fear, acceptance and commitment.[30] It's entirely normal for people to go through a period of emotional adjustment as they come to terms with change – even when change has positive ramifications. Whatever the cause of the change, people generally respond in similar ways. Initially, they respond with shock or denial as they deal with the change to their status quo. They then experience either anger or fear as they realize the extent of the disruption that the change brings, before progressing to acceptance and the acknowledgement that the change is inevitable. The final stage is commitment, when the person is bought in to the change and their focus is on rebuilding. The secret to adapting effectively to change is to learn to how to accelerate through the Change Curve.

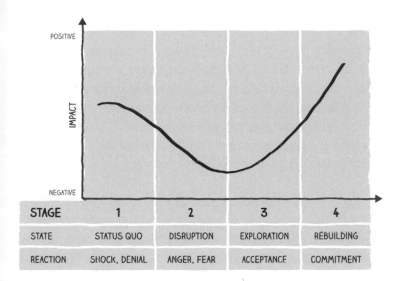

STAGE	1	2	3	4
STATE	STATUS QUO	DISRUPTION	EXPLORATION	REBUILDING
REACTION	SHOCK, DENIAL	ANGER, FEAR	ACCEPTANCE	COMMITMENT

The following steps will help you boost your adaptability. The first step is to change your mindset and view change as exciting, not scary. Try to look for the benefits that change can bring. Be open-minded and see it as a learning opportunity. Don't sweat the small stuff – focus on the bigger picture instead. Resist the temptation to play it safe, be flexible and say 'yes' to opportunities that come your way. Whether it's learning Italian, taking up tennis or signing up for an art class, try something new and reap the rewards of greater confidence.

The next step to help you manage uncertainty is to trust your gut feeling. We are often our own worst enemy – talking ourselves out of new opportunities before they've even begun. The secret to embracing change is to stop overanalysing and go with what feels right for you. Going around in circles can result in indecision that leaves you feeling stuck in limbo. Instead, trust your judgement and have the impetus to go for it! If things don't work out like you'd planned, don't panic – just course correct. It's entirely normal to feel off course at some time or another. Perhaps you've tried something that hasn't worked or maybe you feel out of your depth and in your panic zone. Whatever the situation, the secret is to tune in to how you are feeling, be flexible and make adjustments accordingly. By course correcting in this way, you will feel more in control and this will give you the confidence to be an agent of change and keep trying new things going forward.

I often use the metaphor of surfing to help people get a clearer understanding of how to manage change. Picture a surfer riding their biggest wave – they can't control the wave, so they need to know how to negotiate it and keep their balance. It takes real focus and intent to make the most of their time on the board. They know the ride won't last forever but when they wipe out, they need to have the drive to get back up. It's about adopting a can-do mindset, pushing their limits and focusing on their end goal so they can master the next wave. Life is not linear – we all experience a series of waves that knock us off course. As Steve Jobs said, "You can't connect the dots looking forward; you can only connect them looking backward."[31] The secret to success in life is to have the resilience to get back on course and the ambition to ride the next wave.

KEY TAKEAWAYS

- Learn how to adapt to new situations and accept that change is inevitable.
- Try to evolve your mindset and see change as exciting, not scary.
- Be open minded and look at the bigger picture instead of sticking with the tried and tested.
- Say yes to new opportunities – if things don't work out as planned, course correct and make adjustments accordingly.

3. DEVELOPING YOUR OPTIMISM

Optimism is arguably one of the most important emotional intelligence skills of all. Research from Harvard University reveals that higher levels of optimism are linked to longevity and a greater chance of living past 90.[32] Not only does optimism add years to your life, but it's also the single biggest predictor of success. Optimistic people are wealthier, healthier and more successful in their personal and professional lives. People with high levels of optimism have a positive outlook, sense new opportunities and are able to bounce back from adversity. It's about having a glass-half-full attitude to life that encourages you to see the bigger picture. I'm not talking about seeing the world through rose-tinted glasses – it's about being realistically optimistic and looking for the positives in the situation. Optimists thinking creatively to solve problems, rather than dwelling on any negative emotions.

SIX SIGNS YOU ARE AN OPTIMIST
- You embrace the unfamiliar.
- You face reality quickly.
- You are tenacious and adopt a can-do attitude.
- You are instinctive, intuitive and curious.
- You work hard to stay productive.
- You focus on the task, not negative emotions.

Pessimists, on the other hand, focus on the negatives of a situation, worry about the future and are easily discouraged from trying new things.

COMMON NEGATIVE THOUGHT PATTERNS

- **Overgeneralizing:** believing "it's never going to work" or "nothing I try works out".
- **Personalization:** taking things too personally or comparing yourself to others negatively.
- **Catastrophizing:** focusing on the worst-case scenario.
- **Selective seeing:** only looking at the negatives in a situation.
- **Perfectionism:** expecting higher standards of yourself than others.

The great news is that you don't need to be a natural born optimist – it takes just 21 days to retrain your brain to be more optimistic.[33] Below are three ideas to help you boost your optimism.

FLIP NEGATIVES INTO POSITIVES

As humans, we're hardwired to be more negative than positive. There is an evolutionary basis for this – it helps us survive threats and manage risk. However, it also means that when circumstances don't turn out like we'd hoped, it's easy to fall into a downward spiral of negative thoughts. In extreme cases, we can start catastrophizing by imagining worst-case scenarios. Optimistic people, on the other hand, have the ability to reframe negative thoughts into positive ones. By avoiding black-and-white thinking and finding shades of grey instead, you are more likely to find the benefit in a situation. It's about challenging your disbelief so that instead of thinking, "I will never get a promotion," you ask yourself, "What can I do to increase my chances of getting promoted?"

CHANGE THE WAY YOU THINK ABOUT FAILURE

Optimists see things as changeable and circumstantial and believe they can make a difference. Pessimists, on the other hand, view things as personal and permanent. When things go wrong, think like an optimist by taking the learnings and moving on. Don't be tempted to blame yourself or take things personally. Keep a sense of perspective, pick yourself up and dust yourself down. When you're faced with a setback, don't sit in the doldrums – think creatively and be solution orientated instead. Look to the horizon and seek opportunities to find a new way forward. For example, if you didn't get the promotion you hoped for you, ask yourself instead, "What can I learn from this to help me get promoted in the future?"

VISUALIZE POSITIVE OUTCOMES

Athletes use visualization techniques to help them achieve their peak performance. This technique can be equally powerful in all aspects of your personal and professional life. Instead of using your imagination to think up worst-case scenarios, picture what success looks like to you – this could be making a great impression at your next team meeting, signing the contract for a new job or crossing the finish line at your first marathon. Visualizing the best outcomes in this way will help rewire your brain and boost your positive thinking. Also, remember that optimism is contagious. Human beings like to mirror each other's behaviour.

Whenever possible, surround yourself with people who have a can-do attitude and banish any naysayers.

Developing your optimism will help set you up for success in life. However, it's important to avoid the pitfalls of overplayed optimism:
- Dismissing negative feelings or concerns of others.
- Moving too quickly into 'problem-solving mode' and action planning.
- Feeling empathy internally but not showing it outwardly.
- Indulging in blind optimism – not considering what could go wrong and/or not developing strategies to mitigate any risk.

KEY TAKEAWAYS

- Optimism is the single biggest predictor of success.
- Optimists have a positive outlook, sense new opportunities and are able to bounce back from adversity.
- Pessimists focus on the negatives of a situation, worry about the future and are easily discouraged from trying new things.
- Retrain your brain to be more optimistic by flipping negatives into positives, thinking creatively and visualizing positive outcomes.
- Change the way you view failure by taking the learnings from any setbacks and moving forward.
- Be realistically optimistic.

4. MANAGING YOUR WORK-LIFE BALANCE

A healthy work-life balance will mean different things to different people. It's not about dividing your time equally between your professional and personal life. It's about discovering and managing the right balance for you at a particular time in your life. This balance is constantly shifting. What works for you when you are in your early 20s and starting out in your career may be very different from the balance you crave in your mid-30s when you are trying to juggle the demands of work and family. You need to constantly calibrate your work-life balance and set your own rules as you move through your 20s, 30s, 40s, 50s and 60s so you can actively manage your energy levels. What is certain is that finding a good work-life fit will reduces stress, lower your risk of burnout, and improve your health and sense of well-being.

I firmly believe that it's impossible to separate the *home you* from the *work you*. The need for this became apparent to many people during the pandemic, when the boundaries between our professional and personal lives blurred as a result of the rise in remote working. It's more helpful to look at yourself as a whole person. In order to understand how to strike the right balance, you need to examine the eight facets of your life: business/ career, money, health, friends and family, love and romance, personal development, fun and relaxation, and personal and spiritual growth. By prioritizing the areas that are most important to you, you can take practical steps to manage your bandwidth, sustain your energy and keep your life in balance.

THE WHEEL OF LIFE

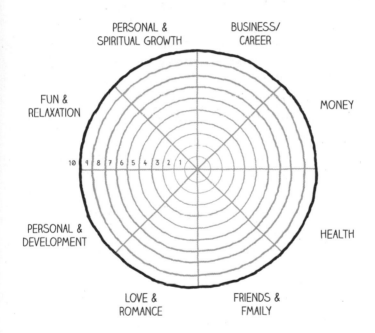

EXERCISE

Use the Wheel of Life to help you identify the areas of your life that are most important to you:

1. Evaluate each area and ask yourself: Where you are now? Give yourself a score out of 10, with 10 out of 10 being totally happy and satisfied with this area.
2. Choose one area you'd like to start working on and write down some bullet points describing what 10 out of 10 would look like to you.
3. Next, write down *why* it's important to work on this area – what difference would it make to improve your score?
4. Identify the one action you could take within the next 24 hours to improve this area of your life, then brainstorm all the possible actions you *could* take over the longer term to help you move closer to scoring a 10 out of 10.
5. Finally, make a shortlist from all of your ideas and choose a couple of next steps you *will* commit to going forward.

You can then repeat this process by focusing on the next area of your life that you believe needs your attention. Once you have your shortlist, follow the practical advice below to help you improve your work–life balance.

Following are some practical steps you can take to help you manage your work-life balance.

FOCUS ON THE SOLUTION, NOT THE PROBLEM

Adopt a positive mindset. Don't see work-life balance as a problem – instead, feel how you have lots of positive choices to make in your life. Use the information you have gathered from the Wheel of Life to help you creatively think of a way forward.

TAKE CONTROL OF YOUR TIME

Think about how you spend your time – pick a day of the week you'd like to review and be specific about how you typically spend that day. Decide what you want to spend your time on and how much time you want to spend on it. Identify an action you can take to help you close the gap between where you are now and where you want to be.

LEARN TO SAY NO

Be more assertive and say no. This will help you if you constantly do favours for others but struggle to ask for help in return. Say no to your smartphone – have boundaries for work and leisure so you don't find yourself reading your work emails before you go to sleep at night.

FOCUS ON YOURSELF

Decide what activities or relaxation time you want to build into your life. Don't feel guilty about doing this – remember that when you're happy and relaxed, your friends and family will feel the benefit. Whether it's doing more exercise, taking up a new hobby or meeting friends for a drink, find ways to carve out some 'me time.'

IDENTIFY ANY MAJOR CHANGES THAT NEED TO TAKE PLACE

For some people, a poor work-life balance comes from simply being in the wrong job. It's tiring and stressful being in a job that doesn't motivate you or play to your strengths. Take the time to identify your true passion and understand your career motivators (more about this in the next section!) Career coaching can also help you identify the right path to find more meaningful work.

WORK SMARTER, NOT HARDER

Refer back to the Four Ds (Do, Delay, Drop and Delegate) in Part Two and be brutal with your to-do list. Decide what you want to achieve by prioritizing what's really important to you. Break it down so that you just have two or three things that you're going to do today. It's much less daunting than having a massive list for the next few weeks or months. Force yourself to identify the items that don't add value and can be eliminated altogether.

BE PRESENT IN THE MOMENT

Channel your energy into whatever you're doing at the present time. As a working parent, I always reminded myself to focus on quality, not quantity. If you're playing with the kids, listen attentively to them. It's much better to have 30-minute periods of dedicated time dotted through the day being *really present*, instead of spending all day with them but not really giving them any undivided attention. If you are at work, be present and focus on the task at hand – don't feel guilty about what's happening at home. This will boost your sense of calm and reduce the stress of feeling you should be somewhere else, doing something else.

By following these steps on a daily basis, you will quickly reap the rewards of a greater sense of achievement and an improved work-life balance. The Japanese concept of *ikigai* is another helpful way to find balance so you can lead a happy and meaningful life.[34] As the diagram below shows, the concept consists of four key areas:

- What you love doing.
- What you are good at.
- What the world needs.
- What you can be paid for.

According to the *ikigai* model, the secret to a happy working life is finding synergy between what you love to do and what you can be paid for. So, use the knowledge you have gathered about yourself so far about what truly motivates and drives you (your reason for getting up in the morning). Then combine this with your key skills and strengths before aligning the outcome with work that is valued by others and that will offer you a financial income.

KEY TAKEAWAYS

- Discover the right work-life balance for you by constantly calibrating it throughout your 20s, 30s, 40s, 50s and 60s.
- Use the Wheel of Life tool to help you identify the areas in your life you need to focus on so you can strike the right balance for you.
- Take control of your time and learn to be more assertive by saying no.
- Don't sweat the small stuff – remember it's only small.
- Identify any major changes that you need to make, such as finding a new job or working more flexibly.
- Be present in the moment so you can channel your energy into the task at hand rather than feeling guilty about the things you aren't doing.

5. REACHING YOUR FULL POTENTIAL

The final emotional intelligence skill you need to hone to help you navigate the world around you is self-actualization. This is about achieving what you are truly capable of achieving and realizing your full potential. Self-actualized people are committed to personal growth and becoming the best version of themselves so they can lead a more successful and meaningful life.

Psychologist Abraham Maslow first popularized the term 'self-actualization' when he introduced his Hierarchy of Needs.[35] The basis of his theory is that we are all motivated by our needs as humans being. If we look at the diagram below, we can see that Maslow breaks down human needs into five levels.

SELF-ACTUALIZATION
MORALITY, CREATIVITY, SPONTANEITY, ACCEPTANCE

SELF-ESTEEM
CONFIDENCE, ACHIEVEMENT, RESPECT OF OTHERS

LOVE AND BELONGING
FRIENDSHIP, FAMILY, INTIMACY, SENSE OF CONNECTION

SAFETY AND SECURITY
HEALTH, EMPLOYMENT, PROPERTY, FAMILY AND SOCIAL STABILITY

PHYSIOLOGICAL NEEDS
BREATHING, FOOD, WATER, SHELTER, CLOTHING, SLEEP

According to Maslow, people are motivated by certain needs and these needs must be fulfilled in a specific order. The lowest stage is our physiological needs – these are the essentials we need to survive, such as water, food and air. The second stage is our need for safety, whether it's our health or stability at home and at work. The third stage is our need to belong and includes our relationships with friends, family and colleagues. Stage four is our need for self-esteem and self-confidence. The final stage is self-actualization and embodies our need for personal growth and self-development. Maslow states that the only way in which you can reach your full potential is to satisfy each need in turn, starting from the bottom.

This is an individual process and will vary from person to person. It's about discovering your purpose and finding your passion, for as Maslow said, "A musician must make music, an artist must paint, a poet must write, if he is to be ultimately happy."[36] My definition of happiness is loving what you do and who you do it with. You therefore need to take practical steps to understand what goals you want to achieve to feel truly fulfilled in life. I'm often reminded of this excerpt from Steve Job's speech to graduating students at Stanford:

> Your work is going to fill a large part of your life, and the only way to be truly satisfied is to do what you believe is great work. And the only way to do great work is to love what you do. If you haven't found it yet, keep looking. Don't settle. As with all matters of the heart, you'll know when you find it.[37]

All too often, people find themselves falling into their first job or climbing the next rung on the corporate ladder without really questioning whether they are going in the right direction. It can be easy to feel boxed into a career when, in reality, most of us no longer aspire to a job for life. It can be helpful to think about your career progression over the course of your lifetime. When you first start work, a year in a job can feel a long time, but your sense of time shifts the older you get. By the time you hit your 40s, you'll be questioning how you want to spend your time working for the next 20 or 30 years. With the wisdom of age, we can get a sense of perspective and see the vast array of opportunities available to us if we have the confidence to take them. It's not surprising that in today's world, an increasing number of people are now choosing a portfolio career that allows them to pursue their passion.

So, how do you find work you love? A great place to start is to ask yourself the following questions:

- What gives you energy?
- What would you do for free?
- What would you regret not having tried?
- If you could try someone else's job for the day, what would it be?
- What puts a smile on your face?
- What do you want to be known for?

I'm a big believer that you make your own luck, but you can only do this if you take the time to understand what truly motivates you. By and large, people are motivated by the following nine career drivers:

- **Material rewards:** seeking wealth, possessions and a high standard of living.
- **Influence:** seeking to be in control of people and resources.
- **Meaning:** seeking to do things that are valued for their own sake
- **Creativity:** seeking to innovate and be connected to an original input.
- **Expertise:** seeking a high level of achievement in a specialized field.
- **Affiliation:** seeking rewarding relationships with others at work.
- **Security:** seeking a stable and predictable future.
- **Recognition:** seeking to be respected by other people.
- **Independence:** seeking to be independent and make your own decisions.

The key to becoming self-actualized and finding fulfilment in life is identifying which motivators are the most relevant and important to you.

EXERCISE

Rank the nine motivators so that they are in order of what makes you feel fulfilled and motivated at work. Then look at your top three motivators and consider:

- What does this motivator mean to me?
- What needs to be happening for this motivator to be fulfilled?
- What can I do to enhance my motivation at work?

Now complete the following table.

MY TOP THREE CAREER MOTIVATORS	WHAT THIS MOTIVATOR MEANS TO ME

A powerful way to help you gain a clear perspective and focus on the future is to think about the legacy you want to leave. Carve out some time to reflect on the stamp you want to make on the earth. It can be helpful to picture yourself as a 70- or 80-year-old looking back on your life. Ask yourself what you want to be known for. How would you like to be remembered? Don't just focus on what you do – consider the influence you have on those around you. Use this knowledge to help inspire you to be the best version of yourself. It's about making an active decision to live your life with purpose. As Nelson Mandela so wisely said, "There is no passion to be found playing small – in settling for a life that is less than the one you are capable of living."[38]

KEY TAKEAWAYS

- Develop your self-actualization so you can reach your potential and lead a more meaningful life.
- Refer to Maslow's Hierarchy of Needs to help you identify what steps you need to take to feel self-actualized.
- Use the career motivators exercise to help you understand your drivers, discover your passion and find work you love.
- Think about your legacy and what you want to be remembered for to help you gain perspective and achieve everything you are capable of achieving.

PART FOUR

MANAGING YOUR RELATIONSHIPS

As we've journeyed together through this book, we've explored the core areas that make up emotional intelligence. So far, we've examined the emotional intelligence skills you need to develop to understand yourself, manage your emotions and navigate the world around you. Now, we are going to concentrate on how you put all of this together to help you build strong relationships with others. If we refer again to our definition of emotional intelligence as **a set of emotional and social skills that are most effective at *influencing others***, you can see just how critical this chapter will be in helping you to lead a more successful life. The art of managing your relationships relates to your ability to develop your empathy, build trust and respect, have straightforward conversations and broaden your network.

Human beings are fundamentally social creatures. Since the beginning of time, we have liked to operate in a pack. Even if you're an introvert, you still need to rely on other people for help, as hardly anyone is an individual contributor at work or in life. Once we recognize that we can't be successful on our own, we begin to understand the true value of building emotional capital in others to help us get things done. By valuing other people in this way, and seeing them as assests worthy of investment, you will reap the rewards of strong connections that deliver tangible results. Whatever job you do, learning how to build relationships is undoubtedly one of the most important emotional intelligence skills to master. It's about communicating with emotional intelligence to engage with others and build high-quality relationships. People with high levels of emotional intelligence focus on what they have in common with others rather than noticing the differences. They recognize that everyone brings something to the table. This lays the foundation for a win–win relationship where both parties feel valued and empowered.

Research shows that there are even proven health benefits to building strong relationships with others. You are less likely to suffer with anxiety or depression. Strong relationships can increase your self-esteem and confidence, help you to recover quickly from illness and lead a longer life. They also make you feel happier. Think about someone in your life with whom you have a great relationship. It could be your partner, a colleague or your oldest friend. Imagine you are arranging a day out with them. If you have a good relationship, it is easy to share ideas about where to go and decide on the itinerary. If, on the other hand, you don't feel comfortable with someone, you are less likely to be open and honest ,and this can make organizing the details more challenging. This is where your emotional intelligence comes in – you have to be able to identify how you are feeling about someone so you can recognize the impact you have on others. Only then can you flex your communication style to help build a better relationship with the other person. It can be easy to take relationships for granted – often we put more effort into them when we first meet someone and get lazier as time goes by. This is not surprising. We are time-poor and are hardwired to take shortcuts. But, as this chapter will clearly show, taking the time to invest in relationships is the most important thing you can do to build a successful life.

1. DEVELOPING YOUR EMPATHY

The first step you need to take to manage your relationships with others is to dial up your empathy to be able to see things from someone else's perspective. It's about putting yourself in the other person's shoes so that you can understand what really makes them tick.

People often interpret this to mean you need to 'be nice' to get ahead, but this confuses sympathy with empathy. Sympathy suggests you feel sorry for the other person, whereas empathy is defined as "the ability to share someone else's feelings or experiences by imagining what it would be like to be in that person's situation."[39] People with high levels of empathy are good listeners, they tune in to other people's emotions and they can read the room. While some people do this effortlessly, others find it difficult to connect with people on a personal level. The great news is that empathy is a skill that can be developed over time. So, even if you're not naturally empathetic or don't instinctively think of other people's feelings, there are steps you can take to change this.

BE CURIOUS

I often describe time as the enemy of empathy. We commonly feel we don't have the time to connect with people at a deeper level and understand their particular challenges or pain points. You therefore need to create the bandwidth to think about other people. People with high levels of empathy are genuinely curious about others. This doesn't mean taking on their pain or issues – it's about minimizing your self-interest so you can truly understand how it feels to walk in their shoes. A great way to do this is to ask clever questions that will give you greater insight into what's important to them. These are open questions that start with words such as "how," "what" or "when" and that require descriptive answers. Your aim is to show genuine interest as this will make the other person feel valued. Try to avoid asking "why" as this could come across as judgemental and prevent the other person from opening up to you.

LISTEN ATTENTIVELY

This may sound obvious, but to be empathetic, you need to listen carefully to the other person. In reality this can be easier said than done. There are three levels of listening (see the diagram on page 116):

- **Cosmetic listening:** when you're only pretending to hear what the other person is saying.
- **Selective listening:** when you're only hearing the things you want to hear.
- **Active listening:** draws on all of your emotional intelligence skills so you listen live in the moment.

Listening attentively takes real effort and concentration to read the other person's body language and tone of voice so you can understand the true meaning behind their words. Be present, calm your mind and focus on the person in front of you. Be aware of any barriers that hinder your ability to listen – this could be deeply ingrained beliefs or physical distractions such as background noise or people moving about. Remember, listening is an active process – dial up your self-control to stay focused on what the other person has to say. Follow Steven Covey's advice when he describes the habit of empathetic communication: "Seek first to understand, then to be understood."[40] In other words, avoid the temptation to listen with the intent to reply rather than to understand. Take care not to be transactional in your approach. This is not about ticking the boxes, it's about going deeper and demonstrating genuine interest.

LISTENING WITH EQ

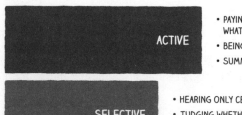

ACTIVE
- PAYING ATTENTION TO UNDERSTAND WHAT THEY MEAN
- BEING PRESENT AND CURIOUS
- SUMMARIZING ACCURATELY

SELECTIVE
- HEARING ONLY CERTAIN PARTS
- JUDGING WHETHER WORTH LISTENING TO
- WAITING TO TALK

COSMETIC
- NOT HEARING OR LISTENING
- LOOKING ELSEWHERE
- DISTRACTED

MAKE A CONNECTION

Once you have developed this capacity to think of others, you need to outwardly show empathy. Build on the information you have gathered by asking the right questions and listening attentively to the answers to establish common ground. If you are struggling to find common ground, try to stay curious and keep asking questions until you find a subject you can agree on or a topic that you both connect with. This will help you to create a balanced relationship based on trust, loyalty and shared experiences. Summarize back what you have heard, using a tone that reflects the content and emotion. The secret to developing empathy is to demonstrate that you can see the world from the other person's point of view in two dimensions: firstly from a cognitive dimension, which means understanding the tasks the other person must perform and the challenges they face, and secondly from an emotional dimension, which means recognizing the other person's emotional experience and feelings.

KEY TAKEAWAYS

- We are social creatures and need to build capital in others to help us get things done.
- Managing your relationships is about developing empathy, building trust and being straightforward.
- Your goal is to focus on what you have in common with other people so you can build a win-win relationship where both parties feel valued and empowered.
- Dial up your empathy to understand other people's perspectives by asking clever questions, listening attentively and finding common ground.
- Outwardly demonstrate this empathy so you can create a balanced relationship based on trust, loyalty and shared experiences.

2. BUILDING TRUST AND RAPPORT

Now that you understand how to harness your empathy, you need to focus on developing your social skills to help you build meaningful relationships. Social skills are based on equality, mutuality and empowerment. Building a relationship is about treating the other person as an equal and expecting to be treated on an equal footing in return so you can work together to get stuff done. People with low levels of social skills struggle to engage well with others. As a consequence, they can appear aloof and disinterested in relationships. In contrast, people with highly developed social skills enjoy others' company and like helping others achieve their goals. It's about earning trust and establishing rapport so that you can build a lasting relationship that delivers for both parties.

The model by Steve Radcliffe on the next page illustrates why relationships are critical to delivering results and getting the job done.[41] The stronger the relationship, the more engaged people will be as they feel listened to and know that their voice counts. This builds a sense of ownership and encourages people to discuss different possibilities and ideas. The next step is to work together to prioritize potential new opportunities, ensuring everyone is committed to following through and taking action. Only when these steps are in place will you be able to work together to deliver real results.

RELATIONSHIPS ARE KEY FOR RESULTS

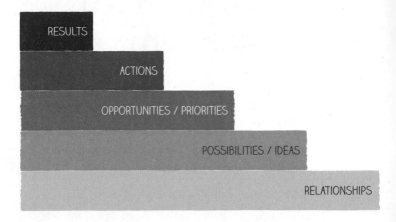

RESULTS

ACTIONS

OPPORTUNITIES / PRIORITIES

POSSIBILITIES / IDEAS

RELATIONSHIPS

The key to building a strong relationship is to be appropriately confident and strike the right balance between arrogance and subservience. If you appear arrogant, this can undermine your ability to build a balanced relationship. It will be human nature for people to want to take you down a peg or two or to find a route around you that stops them having to engage with you. In contrast, if you are subservient, people might not respect you – or, even worse, they may try to take advantage of you. It is the ability to build trust and rapport that lies at the heart of every successful relationship. Zig Ziglar highlighted this when he said, "If people like you, they'll listen to you, if they trust you, they'll do business with you."[42]

Unfortunately, in today's society, trust is on the decline – whether it's trust in the government, the police or the national press. Once lost, trust is hard to rebuild.[43] Warren Buffett highlighted this when he said, "It takes 20 years to build a reputation and five minutes to ruin it. If you think about that, you'll do things differently."[44] This is a powerful reminder never to take relationships for granted. Instead, you need to do things differently by thinking of the various stakeholders in your life and making sure you are committed to managing these relationships. Think of these people as your lifeboat crew – you'll rely on these strong bonds to help get you through the tough times.

Stephen M. R. Covey (son of the more famous Stephen R. Covey) explains the important role trust plays in his book *The Speed of Trust*: "Trust is the glue of life. It's the most essential ingredient in effective communication. It's the foundational principle that holds all relationships."[45] Thankfully, trust is something you can work at and demonstrate though your communication. According to Covey, trust is the act of building credibility based on two components: character and competence. Our character is who we are, while our competence is what we do. Character is based on integrity and intention. Competency is based on capabilities and results. In order to build trust, you need to be honest and have positive intent together with the relevant skills and experience that enable you to deliver results. This means taking a look in the mirror and evaluating your integrity, intention, capabilities and results to identify those areas where you excel and those that require work. Only then will you truly be able to inspire trust in others.

BUILDING TRUST AND RAPPORT WITH DIFFERENT PERSONALITY TYPES

Your ability to communicate with emotional intelligence is key to building trust and rapport. It's about recognizing different people's personality types, respecting them and responding appropriately. Start by using the knowledge you have gathered from page 29 about DISC to help you identify the personality type of the person you are trying to influence. Bear in mind that no one style is better than another – it's about respecting the differences. The next step is to harness your emotional intelligence to flex your own communication style accordingly. This can be easier said than done – following are some dos and don'ts to help you build relationships and deepen your connections with the four different personality types:

D

With D personality types, you need to be brief and to the point, as their preference is to be direct and driven. In a work scenario, focus on results, highlighting the benefits of your ideas and suggest ways to solve any problems. Whenever possible, try not to repeat yourself or go off on a tangent. Avoid making generalizations or statements without evidence to back up your points.

I

If you want to win the hearts and minds of people with an I personality type, you need to give them the time and opportunity to express themselves. These are people who like influencing and persuading others, so you need to show them the big picture and help them turn their ideas into action plans. Your aim should be to communicate in a fun and friendly way. Avoid telling them what to do without their input and don't dwell on lots of detail. They will enjoy sharing personal stories with you and will respond well if you share your feelings.

S

With S personality types, you need to express a genuine interest in them as a person. As they value stability and security, you need to communicate clearly and give them time to adjust to any changes. This means avoiding being confrontational or demanding. Naturally more reserved, they may take their time to open up to you but will respond well to demonstrations of sincere appreciation.

C

As C personality types value compliance and consideration, you need to be more reserved in your approach to building relationships. It can be easier to strike up a conversation about work rather than asking more personal questions. In a workplace scenario, avoid surprising them with new information. Tell them your expectations of them up front, and always give them the pros and cons of different situations.

Whether or not you're a born communicator, you can benefit from following these practical steps to learn how to adapt your communication style so you can build strong relationships with a diverse range of people. After all, as business author John Powell is widely quoted as saying, "Communication works for those who work at it."

EXERCISE

THEIR NAME	STYLE GUESSTIMATE	WHAT WILL I DO?	WHAT WON'T I DO?

Write down a list of the key stakeholders in your life, then try to identify their personality type and the steps you will and won't take to help you build trust and rapport with them. An example could be your boss who is a D personality type. Your aim might be to build a deeper relationship by being more direct and succinct and avoiding having long, drawn-out conversations that could frustrate them.

KEY TAKEAWAYS

- Build trust and rapport by treating the other person as an equal and expecting to be treated on an equal footing in return.
- Develop your social skills by being appropriately confident and striking the right balance between arrogance and subservience.
- Build trust with others through your character and competence: who you are and what you do.
- Use your knowledge of DISC to recognize different people's personality types, respect them and respond appropriately so you can build emotional capital.

3. HAVING STRAIGHTFORWARD CONVERSATIONS

Communicating in a straightforward manner is also critical to building strong relationships with others. Straightforwardness is a core emotional intelligence skill ,as it enables you to have the courage of your convictions and say what needs to be said in an honest and open way. This is important because relationships that stand the test of time are based on respect and reciprocity. If you lack straightforwardness, you will find it difficult to stand up for your own opinion and are more likely to be intimidated. This can create misunderstandings and mistrust and could ultimately lead to a toxic relationship where you feel used or taken for granted.

Many people struggle to develop straightforwardness. Often this is because they don't want to appear to be too direct. It's important to clarify that communicating straightforwardly is not about being dominant and directive. It's about articulating your thoughts and views clearly and concisely while acknowledging that the other person may hold a different view or expectation. Only then will you be able to draw on your assertiveness and self-control to challenge the views of others and say no when the need arises.

HOW TO DEVELOP STRAIGHTFORWARDNESS

Before you take practical steps to develop your straightforwardness, it's helpful to gain insight into where you currently stand. Give yourself an honest appraisal to establish how straightforward you actually are. A great way to do this is to get 360-degree feedback or use an Emotional Capital Report tool, which will help benchmark where you sit.[46] You can then set out to develop a positive mindset by concentrating on the benefits of having straightforward conversations. Don't be tempted to procrastinate and shy away from difficult exchanges. Manage your anxiety by drawing on your self-control to focus on what you can control, not what you can't. A great way to build your confidence is to plan ahead and prepare what you want to say, why you want to say it and the benefits of getting it right. Try not to worry too much about how the other person will react, as this can prevent you from being open and honest. This can be easier said than done, particularly if you are a people pleaser. Rather than worry about being judged, take control of the situation by managing your emotional state.

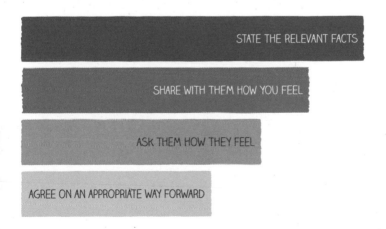

STATE THE RELEVANT FACTS

SHARE WITH THEM HOW YOU FEEL

ASK THEM HOW THEY FEEL

AGREE ON AN APPROPRIATE WAY FORWARD

The diagram on page 127 takes you through the steps you need to take to have a straightforward conversation. When it comes to delivering your message, you need to take a deep breath and have a clear mind. Use your knowledge of both your own and the other's personality type to help you. Whenever possible, try to say your piece first, so that you can communicate what you want to say before you are consumed by the other person's needs. It's important to express your point of view clearly and confidently. Make direct eye contact and use a neutral tone of voice. Try to use simple language and repeat your key message if necessary so the other person understands exactly where you stand. Avoid 'weak speak' – those vague or hackneyed words and phrases such as "hopefully," "potentially" or "I may be wrong but ... " as these inadvertently undermine your position. Instead get to the point quickly and own the message by saying "I've noticed" or "I feel." If you draw on your self-control and talk about your feelings in a calm and collected way, people are more likely to listen to what you have to say. Once you have stated the relevant facts and told the other person how you feel, you need to ask them how they feel in response. Your aim is to understand their perspective by listening empathetically. You can then continue the conversation by drawing on your optimism to be solution orientated so you can agree on a new way forward.

Try to avoid being too blunt, talking at the other person or being tempted to spin the truth. If you are overly straightforward, you need to recognize that the other person may back off. Being straightforward is not about talking in an aggressive way, as this can make the other person feel defensive or respond aggressively in return. If, despite your best-laid plans, you find yourself deferring to others, draw on strategies to help develop your assertiveness.

This could involve visualizing success or role-modelling someone you admire who displays high levels of straightforwardness. Perhaps it's an emotionally intelligent leader or someone from the world of sports who voices their thoughts and beliefs in a confident and honest manner.

USING STRAIGHTFORWARDNESS TO DEAL WITH UNREASONABLE BEHAVIOUR

Unfortunately, as many of us know only too well, not all of the relationships with our stakeholders are positive ones. Based on my experience, incidents of unreasonable behaviour in the workplace are still all too common, whether it's intimidation, discrimination or bullying. It is, therefore, more important than ever to draw on your straightforwardness to learn how to back yourself and call out these examples of unacceptable behaviour.

RECOGNIZE IT

The first step is to recognize when people are throwing curve balls designed to undermine you. Sometimes this behaviour will be deliberate, whereas sometimes the person will do it unwittingly. In either case, you need to spot the unfair comments and tell yourself that this sort of behaviour is always unacceptable. A great way to do this is to think about how children behave if they can't get their own way. This could be stamping their feet or storming out of the room if they aren't allowed out to play. Now use your emotional intelligence to see this through a workplace lens – I'm sure we can all think of a time when a colleague or customer raised their voice or used silence as a way of getting the upper hand.

RESPOND NOT REACT

The next step is to draw on your emotional intelligence to work out the best way to respond to this unreasonable behaviour. Remind yourself that you can't control *their* behaviour but you can control how *you* respond to it. Take a deep breath to help you stay calm and use your self-control to think about how to respond in a measured way rather than reacting in a knee-jerk manner. Giving yourself time to order your thoughts will ensure you get the best possible outcome from your interaction. Above all, avoid responding by text or WhatsApp – the written word is much more open to interpretation and could inadvertently fan the flames.

PUSH BACK

It's important to deal with the intimidation in a situationally appropriate way. Have the courage to call them out and name their behaviour to show that you know what they are trying to do. Level the playing field by showing them that their behaviour or comment is not acceptable. One way to re-establish the balance of power is to use humour to defuse the situation. For example, if your customer greets your proposal with a wall of silence, don't be afraid to say to them, "It seems as though you're giving me the silent treatment!" It's important to say this with the right tone, as your aim should be to defuse rather than fuel the situation.

MOVE ON

Once you've shown the other party you are an equal, draw on your resilience and try not to dwell on the conversation. Don't let their behaviour put you off your stride, or even worse, worry that you might have upset them. Instead focus on what you want to achieve and get back to what the conversation should be about. This could be making a new proposal if you are dealing with a customer, agreeing on next steps if you are talking to a supplier or identifying new ways of working if you are dealing with a colleague.

By drawing on your straightforwardness in this way to tackle unacceptable behaviour head on, you will help to create a culture that fosters inclusion and diversity, where people are open to forming new relationships based on mutual trust and respect.

KEY TAKEAWAYS

- Communicating in a straightforward manner is critical to building strong relationships with others.
- Straightforwardness is having the courage of your convictions so you can say what needs to be said in an honest and open way.
- Boost your straightforwardness by managing your mood, controlling your emotions and drawing on your assertiveness.
- Use your emotional intelligence skills to call out and deal with unreasonable behaviour whenever and wherever it occurs, whether it's intimidation, discrimination or bullying.

4. BROADENING YOUR NETWORK

I'm a big believer that if you love your network, your network will love you. In today's competitive world, the ability to make new connections lies at the heart of success in work and in life. Think of it as casting your net wide so you can broaden your network. If, however, you find the idea of networking daunting, you're certainly not alone. Perhaps it's the thought of having to initiate a conversation with a group of people or maybe you dread getting stuck with the same person for a long time. It can be helpful to remind yourself of the benefits of networking by seeing it as **emotionally intelligent conversations to find a 'fit' and a 'connection' that open up opportunities**. Networking gives you the opportunity to gather intelligence, build your profile and identify the potential for collaboration. It's about adopting a targeted approach, whether it's reconnecting with people you know already, finding introductions through your existing network or proactively connecting with new contacts.

EXERCISE

The chart below will help you prioritize the people you need to contact and the actions you should take to set yourself up for networking success. Your top priority should be people who fit into the top righthand box (for 'known' and 'more influential' people), as they will be the most likely to help you achieve your goals. You should then devote time and effort to connecting with people in the bottom righthand 'unknown' and 'more influential' box, as they will offer you the potential for collaboration. The third step is to think of your existing network and identify the people in the top lefthand 'known' and 'less influential' box to see whether they can help you. Your lowest priority should be people in the bottom lefthand box who are 'unknown' and 'less influential' – they only warrant a light-touch approach to networking.

KNOWN / ESTABLISHED RELATIONSHIP

CONSIDER HOW THEY COULD HELP
- NAME
- ACTION

GET IN TOUCH NOW
- NAME
- ACTION

LESS INFLUENTIAL

MORE INFLUENTIAL

LIGHT-TOUCH EFFORT
- NAME
- ACTION

MAXIMUM EFFORT MAKING CONTACT
- NAME
- ACTION

UNKNOWN / NO RELATIONSHIP

Once you have identified who you want to connect with, it's time to dig deep and take the plunge. As the saying goes, you never get a second chance to make a first impression, so be proactive and take steps to make a strong impression. In my experience, it takes just a quick glance, maybe three seconds, for someone to evaluate you when you meet for the first time. In this short time, the other person forms an opinion about you based on your appearance, body language, demeanour and mannerisms. These first impressions can be nearly impossible to reverse or undo, making those first encounters extremely important, as they set the tone for all the relationships that follow. The secret to making a strong first impression is to adopt a confident approach. Judge the person and the situation and introduce yourself with your name and role. Your goal is to establish credibility and project confidence, not arrogance.

One of the main reasons people shy away from capitalizing on networking opportunities is because they worry about how to make small talk. The key to setting yourself up for success is to have something to say, so prepare and practise your 'elevator pitch' (a brief and memorable description to introduce who you are and what you do) ahead of time to help capture their attention and get your message across clearly and succinctly. Your aim is to differentiate yourself from others, claiming maximum airspace in a concise and compelling way. The next step is to be interested in what the other person has to say. A great way to do this is to ask questions to understand their particular challenges or areas of interest. For example, "Is there anything specific you are hoping to achieve from this event?" or "Tell me more about your role/department/organization?" or "What do you see as your biggest opportunities/challenges?"

You should then draw on your emotional intelligence to listen with empathy to their response. Your goal is to make an authentic connection with the other person and have the confidence to communicate the real you. Let your personality shine. By being authentic, you are more likely to appear credible and trustworthy.

Finally, it may sound obvious but remember to keep in touch by agreeing the best way to stay connected. At the end of a networking event, it can be all too tempting to connect on LinkedIn and leave it at that. So whenever possible, make sure you follow up on your conversation and start the process of building a relationship – for example, "Let's swap contact details and stay in touch about ... " or "What's the best way of arranging a meeting?" or "I'll introduce you to my colleague." This could mean picking up the phone or sending an email. However, don't bombard them – your aim is to show them how you can help them, not to be an irritation! I hope that by being interested and interesting, giving your time and making genuine connections, you will learn to love networking and reap the rewards of increased confidence and a wider network that offers you new opportunities.

As this part of the book has shown, relationships don't just happen. They take commitment and effort. One of the most important pieces of advice that I give my clients is to be generous with their time. Generally, there are three types of people in life – takers, matchers and givers. A taker will always position themselves at the centre of the agenda, a matcher will adopt a 'you scratch my back and I'll scratch yours' approach and a giver will be prepared to go the extra mile on your behalf. In life what goes around tends to come around, so whenever possible try to invest your time with the other person – you don't have to give something away for free but try to be appropriately giving and you will reap the rewards of improved relationships and greater success in life. I can't emphasize this enough – it's about paying it forward. People mirror people. By cultivating relationships and surrounding yourself with radiators rather than drains, you are sure to build strong relationships that deliver real results.

Finally, in this digital age, never underestimate the importance of meeting face to face to manage your relationships with your stakeholders. You can only achieve so much over Zoom or email. Anything that involves collaborating, creativity, conflict, confidentiality and developing chemistry is better done in person. They are called interpersonal skills for a reason, so try to save email, Slack and WhatsApp for confirmation, not communication.

KEY TAKEAWAYS

- Remind yourself that if you love your network, your network will love you.
- Adopt a targeted approach to networking: reconnect with people you know already, find introductions through your existing network and proactively connect with new contacts.
- Make a strong first impression by establishing credibility and projecting confidence, not arrogance.
- Prepare and practise your elevator pitch so you can capture the other person's attention.
- Be interested and interesting to help you find common ground and make an authentic connection.
- Remember to follow up with any new connections, whether by phone or email, to start building a new relationship.
- Be generous with your time and put the effort into managing your relationships so you can benefit from increased success.
- Don't underestimate the importance of meeting face to face: use email and WhatsApp for confirmation, not communication.

PART FIVE

LIVING LIFE
WITH EMOTIONAL
INTELLIGENCE

1. SETTING YOURSELF UP FOR SUCCESS

Congratulations on reaching the final part of *The Emotional Intelligence Book*. I hope you now have a deep understanding of exactly what emotional intelligence is and the specific skills you need to develop to set yourself up for success in life. We've looked in detail at the four core areas that make up emotional intelligence: knowing yourself (self-awareness), managing yourself (self-control, self-confidence and self-reliance), navigating the world around you (ambition, adaptability, optimism, work-life balance and self-actualization) and managing your relationships (empathy, social skills and straightforwardness). The next step to becoming truly emotionally intelligent is to combine these skills in a balanced way so you can become the best version of yourself.

Emotional intelligence is not just an add-on – it is intrinsic to how you should go about everything in life. It's about putting emphasis on the power of emotions and feelings rather than just focusing on facts and empirical knowledge. I believe this is best summed up by the mantra "I feel, therefore I am." As I mentioned in the introduction, your innate level of emotional intelligence will increase over the course of your lifetime. The secret to harnessing the power of emotional intelligence is to fast-track it by actively developing these skills on a daily basis. It's about learning from the experiences you have and the various people you meet. To truly excel in life, you need a balance of strengths across all the different emotional intelligence competencies. Use the knowledge you have gathered by reading this book and completing the various exercises to recognize your super-strengths and your areas for development. Perhaps you are great at building relationships but struggle with self-control, or maybe you have the courage of your convictions but focus too much on the negatives?

It's important to bear in mind that an overplayed strength can become a performance risk. You therefore need to constantly calibrate these skills. This means drawing on your self-awareness to prioritize the specific skills you need to master to create this sense of balance. Don't just think about your emotional intelligence skills in the context of workplace scenarios – consider the interconnectivity of these skills in social and informal settings as well. Only then can you take practical steps to combine your emotional intelligence with your technical skills and actual intelligence to achieve your full potential.

2. TRACKING YOUR PROGRESS

As this book has clearly shown, there is nothing 'soft' about emotional intelligence skills – they are some of the hardest to master. It's about taking a conscious and disciplined approach to developing your skill set. I'd love to say that just by reading this book, you have become more emotionally intelligent. Unfortunately, changing your behaviour takes ambition, hard work and commitment. You need to be in it for the long haul – but the benefits are worth it! So, resist the temptation to put this book on the shelf or in a drawer. Instead, keep it nearby and use it as a guide to support you on your journey. Use the exercises it contains to help you track your progress by repeating them at regular intervals as necessary. After all, what gets measured gets done.

Begin by focusing on those things you are going to start, stop and continue (see page 70). A great way to build momentum is to start small with low-risk situations. When you've mastered an easy one, pick something harder. Try to embed these new habits and behaviours by adopting the principle of Plan, Do and Review (see Part Two). If you have a specific situation in mind, take the time to plan the approach you are going to take, put your plan into action, then review how it went. Ask yourself what worked well and what you would do differently next time.

Keeping a journal is another tool that can help you track your progress. It can be useful to think about the various interactions you have during your day – either good or bad. Keep in mind the core emotional intelligence skills you are working on and whether you overcame any challenges. Reflect on your entries over time to see if you can spot any trends or situations that you found particularly difficult as well as where there have been obvious improvements. Use these trends to help you predict how you will feel and behave in future situations. This will help to increase your self-awareness and allow you to focus more closely on your strengths and areas for development.

It's important to keep a sense of perspective as you develop your new skills. Don't just focus on the end game – remember to celebrate the small wins along the way, as this will boost your motivation. Acknowledging these small wins allows you to track your progress and appreciate how far you have come on your journey to becoming more emotionally intelligent. It's about positive reinforcement and reminding yourself of the benefit you are getting from honing these skills – whether it's being able to push back and say no when you need to or having the confidence to attend your first networking event. A powerful way to embed these changes in behaviour is to give yourself a pat on the back for a job well done. Rewarding yourself for your achievement, perhaps by treating yourself with a coffee or a meal out, will train your brain to do the same thing again. Be kind to yourself and recognize your own personal victory.

3. SETTING NEW GOALS

Given today's levels of uncertainty and change, emotional intelligence is the game changer that allows you to reinvent yourself and keep growing as an individual. Don't be tempted to take it for granted or underestimate its importance. Keep it front of mind and remind yourself that developing your emotional intelligence is a lifelong process. You will want different things at different stages in your life. Your goal should be brave and front-footed as you continually evolve to cope with what life throws at you.

Take another look at the Wheel of Life (see page 97) and focus on setting those goals that will help you feel fulfilled at the current time. Even if you have a sense of fulfilment now, you might take on another challenge that moves everything out of kilter. It's about staying in your Learning Zone (see page 33), where you can make the most of new opportunities. Remember, life is not a dress rehearsal. The more effort you put into developing your emotional intelligence skills, the more successful you will become. Only then will you move along the learning pathway from conscious competence to unconscious competence (see page 13), where your emotional intelligence skills are so embedded they feel second nature.

The secret to achieving your goals is to stay positive and not give up. It's about adopting a growth mentality. Follow the example of Thomas Edison, who took 10,000 attempts to make the light bulb. When he was questioned about this he said, "I have not failed 10,000 times – I've successfully found 10,000 ways that will not work."[47] It's about taking the learnings from any setbacks and moving forward. Think back to the Change Curve (see page 89): you need to be in the Rebuilding state, where you are committed to change. Only then can you become the best version of yourself.

One final piece of advice – don't be tempted to compare yourself to others. Everyone is wonderfully unique. You need to work out what success means to you. For some people it might be financial freedom; for others it could be finding work with meaning. By developing your emotional intelligence in an authentic way, you'll learn to differentiate yourself and thrive in all areas of your life. I'll leave you with some more words commonly attributed to one of my favourite authors, Maya Angelou, that I hope will inspire you to lead a more emotionally intelligent life: "My mission in life is not to merely survive, but to thrive; and to do so with some passion, some compassion, some humour and some style."[48]

KEY TAKEAWAYS

Here's a final reminder of the steps you need to take to dial up your emotional intelligence and lead a more successful life:

- Your goal is to combine your emotional intelligence skills in a balanced way so you can become the best version of yourself.
- Fast-track your emotional intelligence by practising these skills on a daily basis.
- Don't just focus on developing your skills in the workplace – remember to hone them in social and informal situations as well.
- Adopt a disciplined approach to developing your skill set so you can measure your progress over time.
- Use this book as a guide to support you on your journey to becoming more emotionally intelligent – refer to the top tips and repeat the relevant exercises as necessary.

- Start with small, low-risk situations and when you've mastered these, move on to more challenging ones.
- Adopt the principle of Plan, Do and Review to help you keep raising the bar.
- Journaling can help you reflect on how you are doing and keep you on track as you develop these new skills.
- Celebrate the small wins – this positive reinforcement will help you stay motivated and focused over the long term.
- Remember that developing your emotional intelligence is a lifelong process – don't be tempted to take it for granted.
- Learn how to develop your emotional intelligence in an authentic way to help you thrive in all areas of your life.

NOTES

1. Daniel Goleman, *Emotional Intelligence: Why It Can Matter More than IQ* (London: Bloomsbury, 1996).

2. Emily B. H. Treichler, Barton W. Palmer, Tsung-Chin Wu, Michael L. Thomas, Xin M. Tu, Rebecca Daly, Ellen E. Lee and Dilip V. Jeste, "Women and Men Differ in Relative Strengths in Wisdom Profiles: A Study of 659 Adults Across the Lifespan," *Frontiers in Psychology* 12 (2021), accessed 6 July 2023, https://doi.org/10.3389/fpsyg.2021.769294.

3. M. Newman, Emotional Capital Inventory, Technical Manual 2007

4. Jennifer S Learner, Ye Li, Piercarlo Valdesolo and Karim S. Kassam, "Emotion and Decision Making," *Annual Review of Psychology* 66 (2015): 799–823.

5. Charles Mann, *A Study of Engineering Education* (Boston, MA: Merrymount Press, 1918).

6. https://www.exceptionalleaderslab.com/blogs/its-time-to-give-noel-burch-some-credit

7. Abraham Maslow, "A Theory of Human Motivation," *Psychological Review* 50, no. 4 (1943): 370–396.

8. Robert Plutchik *Emotion: Theory, Research, and Experience:* Vol. 1. *Theories of Emotion* (New York: Academic, 1980).

9. To access learning zone tool, visit https://positivepsychology.com/comfort-zone/

10. Joseph Luft and Harry Ingham, "The Johari Window, a Graphic Model of Interpersonal Awareness," in *Proceedings of the Western Training Laboratory in Group Development* (Los Angeles: University of California, Los Angeles, 1955).

11. Anne Trafton, "In the Blink of an Eye" (MIT News), last modified 16 January 2014, https://news.mit.edu/2014/in-the-blink-of-an-eye-0116.

12. Albert Mehrabian, *Silent Messages: Implicit Communication of Emotions and Attitude* (Belmont, CA: Wadsworth, 1971).

13. Cyril Northcote Parkinson, "Parkinson's Law," *The Economist*, 19 November 1955.

14. Matthew A. Killingsworth and Daniel T. Gilbert, "A Wandering Mind is an Unhappy Mind," *Science* 330, no. 6006 (2010): 932.

15. Reported by Kevin McSpadden, "You Now Have a Shorter Attention Span than a Goldfish" (*Time*), last modified 14 May 2015, https://time.com/3858309/attention-spans-goldfish.

16. Daniel Goleman, *Focus: The Hidden Driver of Excellence* (New York: HarperCollins, 2013).

17. Jack Canfied, *The Power of Focus* (London: Vermilion, 2001).

18. Stephen Karpman, "Fairy Tales and Script Drama Analysis," *Transactional Analysis Bulletin* 7, no. 26 (1968): 39–43.

19. Erica Martin, "6 Pilot Rules that Everyone Should Live By" (*Phoenix East Aviation*), last modified 6 August 2013, https://pea.com/blog/posts/6-pilot-rules-that-everyone-should-live-by.

20. John Carlin, *Invictus: Nelson Mandela and the Game that Made a Nation*, (London: Penguin Books, 2009)

21. Taiichi Ohno, *Toyota Production System: Beyond Large-Scale Production* (Cambridge, MA: Productivity Press, 1988).

22. Gill Corkindale, "Overcoming Imposter Syndrome" (*Harvard Business Review*), last modified 7 May 2008, https://hbr.org/2008/05/overcoming-imposter-syndrome.

23. Jaruwan Sakulku and James Alexander, "The Impostor Phenomenon," *International Journal of Behavioral Science* 6, no. 1 (2011): 73–92.

24. Quoted in Michelle Kerrigan, "7 Signs You Suffer from the Impostor Syndrome" (*Business Insider*), last modified 29 October 2013, https://www.businessinsider.com/signs-you-suffer-from-the-impostor-syndrome-2013-10.

25. "Michelle Obama Tells London School She Still Has Imposter Syndrome" (*The Guardian*), last modified 3rd December 2018, https://www.theguardian.com/us-news/2018/dec/03/ michelle-obama-tells-london-school-she-still-has-imposter-syndrome

26. "Why Sir Richard Branson is the World's Most Beloved Billionaire" (*The CEO Magazine*), last modified 21 July 2022, https://www. theceomagazine.com/business/coverstory/richard-branson-billionaire/

27. "Live Updates: Zelenskyy Declines US Offer to Evacuate Kyiv" (Associated Press), last modified 26 February 2022, https://apnews.com/article/ russia-ukraine-business-europe-united-nations-kyiv-6ccba0905f187199 2b93712d3585f548.

28. Sheryl Sandberg, *Lean In: Women, Work, and the Will to Lead* (New York: Knopf Doubleday, 2013

29. Michelle Obama, *Becoming*, (London: Penguin Books, 2018)

30. Elisabeth Kübler-Ross, *On Death and Dying* (New York: Simon & Schuster, 1969).

31. "'You've got to find what you love,' Jobs says" (Stanford News), last modified 12 June 2005, https://news.stanford.edu/2005/06/12/ youve-got-find-love-jobs-says.

32. Hayama Kogi, Claudia Trudel-Fitzgerald, Lewina O. Lee, Peter James, Candyce Kroenke, Lorena Garcia, Aladdin H. Shadyab, Elena Salmoirago-Blotcher, JoAnn E. Manson, Francine Grodstein and Laura D. Kubzansky, "Optimism, Lifestyle, and Longevity in a Racially Diverse Cohort of Women," *Journal of the American Geriatrics Society* 70, no. 10 (2022): 2793–2804.

33. Shawn Achor, *The Happiness Advantage: The Seven Principles of Positive Psychology that Fuel Success and Performance at Work* (London: Virgin, 2010).

34. Héctor García and Francesc Miralles, *Ikigai: The Japanese Secret to a Long and Happy Life* (New York: Penguin, 2017).

35. Abraham Maslow, "A Theory of Human Motivation," *Psychological Review* 50, no. 4 (1943): 370–396.

36. Abraham Maslow, "A Theory of Human Motivation," *Psychological Review* 50, no. 4 (1943): 382.

37. "'You've got to find what you love,' Jobs says" (*Stanford News*), last modified 12 June 2005, https://news.stanford.edu/2005/06/12/youve-got-find-love-jobs-says.

38. Nelson Mandela, *Long Walk to Freedom* (London: Little, Brown, 1994),

39. "Empathy" (*Cambridge Dictionary*), accessed 8 July 2023, https://dictionary.cambridge.org/dictionary/english/empathy.

40. Stephen Covey, *The 7 Habits of Highly Effective People* (London: Simon & Schuster, 1989).

41. Steve Radcliffe, *Future, Engage, Deliver: The Essential Guide to Your Leadership* (Leicester: Matador, 2008)

42. Zig Ziglar, *See You At The Top* (Louisiana USA: Pelican Books 1975)

43. Quoted by Christine Lagarde in "There's a reason for the lack of trust in government and business", (*IMF*), last modified May 2018, https://www.imf.org/en/Blogs/Articles/2018/05/04/theres-a-reason-for-the-lack-of-trust-in-government-and-business-corruption

44. Quoted in James Berman, "The Three Essential Warren Buffett Quotes to Live By" (*Forbes*), last modified 20 April 2014, https://www.forbes.com/sites/jamesberman/2014/04/20/the-three-essential-warren-buffett-quotes-to-live-by.

45. Stephen M. R. Covey, *The Speed of Trust* (London: Simon & Schuster, 2006)

46. You can measure your emotional intelligence skills with an Emotional Capital Report assessment through https://www.rochemartin.com.

47. Quoted by Erica R. Hendry, "7 Epic Fails Brought to You by the Genius Mind of Thomas Edison" (*Smithsonian Magazine*), last modified 20 November 2013, https://www.smithsonianmag.com/innovation/7-epic-fails-brought-to-you-by-the-genius-mind-of-thomas-edison-180947786.

48. 47 As quoted from "The 3 Lessons Maya Angelou Taught Us About Coping" (*Huff Post*), last modified August 2014, https://www.huffpost.com/entry/maya-angelou-legacy_b_5479355

FURTHER READING

"A Theory of Human Motivation," Abraham Maslow, *Psychological Review* 50, no. 4 (1943): 370–396

Confessions of a Public Speaker, Scott Berkun (Farnham: O'Reilly, 2010)

"Do Schools Kill Creativity?" Ken Robinson (TED, 2006), accessed 6 July 2021, https://www.ted.com/talks/sir_ken_robinson_do_schools_kill_creativity/c

Drive: The Surprising Truth about What Motivates Us, Daniel Pink (New York: Riverhead Books, 2011)

Eat that Frog: 21 Great Ways to Stop Procrastinating and Get More Done in Less Time, Brian Tracy (San Francisco: Berrett-Koehler, 2001)

Emotional Capitalists: The Ultimate Guide to Developing Emotional Intelligence for Leaders, Martyn Newman (Milton, Queensland: John Wiley & Sons, 2007)

Emotional Intelligence: Why It Can Matter More than IQ, Daniel Goleman (London: Bloomsbury, 1996)

Emotional Intelligence Coaching, Stephen Neale, Lisa Spencer-Arnell and Liz Wilson (London: Kogan Page, 2011)

Focus: The Hidden Driver of Excellence, Daniel Goleman (New York: HarperCollins, 2013)

Future, Engage, Deliver: The Essential Guide to Your Leadership, Steve Radcliffe (Leicester: Matador, 2008)

Grace under Pressure: A Masterclass in Public Speaking, Lisa Wentz (New York: LID Publishing, 2019)

How to Own the Room: Women and the Art of Brilliant Speaking, Viv Groskop (London: Bantam Press, 2018)

How to Win Friends and Influence People, Dale Carnegie
(New York: Simon & Schuster, 1936)

Lean In: Women, Work, and the Will to Lead, Sheryl Sandberg
(New York: Knopf Doubleday, 2013)

Mindset: The New Psychology of Success, Carol Dweck
(New York: Ballantine Books, 2006)

Silent Messages: Implicit Communication of Emotions and Attitude,
Albert Mehrabian (Belmont, CA: Wadsworth, 1971)

Start with Why: How Great Leaders Inspire Everyone to Take Action,
Simon Sinek (London: Portfolio, 2009)

"Teach Every Child about Food," Jamie Oliver (TED Talk,
2010), accessed 6 July 2023, https://www.ted.com/talks/
jamie_oliver_teach_every_child_about_food

The Challenger Sale: How to Take Control of the Customer Conversation,
Matthew Dixon and Brent Adamson (London: Portfolio, 2011)

The Chimp Paradox, Steve Peters (London: Vermillion, 2012)

The Coaching Book: Practical Steps to Becoming a Confident Coach,
Nicole Soames (London: LID Publishing, 2019)

The Coaching Habit, Michael Bungay Stanier (Toronto: Box of Crayons
Press, 2016)

The Effective Executive, Peter Drucker (New York: Harper & Row, 1967)

The Gifts of Imperfection, Brené Brown (City Center, MN: Hazelden, 2010)

The Influence Book: Practical Steps to Becoming a Strong Influencer,
Nicole Soames (London: LID Publishing, 2018)

The Inner Game of Tennis, W. Timothy Gallwey (New York: Random House, 1974)

The Inner Game of Work, W. Timothy Gallwey (New York: Random House, 2000)

The Mindfulness Book: Practical Ways to Lead a More Mindful Life,
Martyn Newman (London: LID Publishing, 2016)

The Negotiation Book: Practical Steps to Becoming a Master Negotiator, Nicole Soames (London: LID Publishing, 2017)

The Power of Focus, Jack Canfield (London: Vermillon, 2001)

The Presentation Secrets of Steve Jobs, Carmine Gallo (New York: McGraw-Hill, 2009)

The Presenting Book: Practical Steps on How to Make a Great Impression, Nicole Soames (London: LID Publishing, 2020)

The 7 Habits of Highly Effective People, Stephen Covey (London: Simon & Schuster, 1989)

ACKNOWLEDGEMENTS

Writing a book on the power of emotional intelligence has long been an important goal for me. As a trainer, coach and emotional intelligence practitioner, I'm fortunate enough to have my own personal toolkit to help me develop my emotional intelligence. I'm by no means perfect, but I actively put the theory into practice on a daily basis so I can become the very best version of myself. This is why I was so determined to share my knowledge and expertise with others in a book. I'm passionate about encouraging everyone to work on themselves so they can lead a more successful life.

Thanks to my clients throughout the world who constantly inspire me in my work. A special mention needs to go to my fabulous team at Diadem and of course my wonderful family – my husband, James, and daughters, Talya and Amelie. Finally, thanks to Martin Liu and the team at LID Publishing for their help and support with book number five.

ABOUT THE AUTHOR

NICOLE SOAMES is a highly qualified executive coach, commercial skills trainer and emotional intelligence practitioner. She gained extensive commercial experience from 12 years managing large sales teams at Unilever and United Biscuits, followed by more than 18 years developing and delivering training programmes around the world. In 2009 Nicole founded Diadem, a commercial and leadership skills training and coaching company. With many hundreds of clients across the globe, Diadem has helped thousands of people become *commercial athletes* in influencing and selling, negotiation, account management, marketing, presenting, strategy, coaching, leadership and management.

Nicole's charismatic and energetic communication style and ability to drive change enable people from a diverse range of organizations to think and act outside their comfort zone and unlock their true potential. Nicole is also the author of the bestselling *The Coaching Book*, *The Influence Book*, *The Presenting Book* and *The Negotiation Book*, all in the Concise Advice series from LID Business Media. For more information about Nicole's books visit www.nicolesoamesbooks.com.

Connect with Nicole Soames:
LinkedIn – **nicolesoamesatdiadem**
X – **@NicoleSAuthor**

Get in touch regarding you or your team at
www.diademperformance.com

BY THE SAME AUTHOR

ISBN: 978-1-911687-98-6

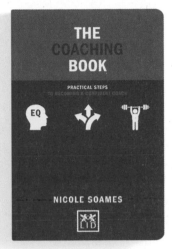

ISBN: 978-1-912555-53-6

ISBN: 978-1-911498-42-1

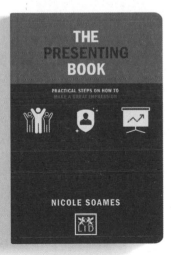

ISBN: 978-1-912555-71-0